REINVENTING YOURSELF AT ANY AGE

A Practical and Spiritual Instruction (Wo)manual

Reinventing Yourself at Any Age:
A Practical and Spiritual Instruction (Wo)manual

By Trudy R. Tobias, MSW, LCSW

Disclaimer: This book is not meant to be a replacement for therapy. If you feel that you cannot make these changes alone, I encourage you to get the professional support you need from either a professional mental health therapist or a life coach. If, after reading the book, you would like me to work with you as your professional therapist or life coach, please contact me at;

Trudy@truestlifecoaching.com,
Trudy@truestlifecounseling.com,
or 336-763-4611.

To maintain confidentiality of my clients, their names have been changed, but not their stories. Other identifying information, such as place of employment, has deliberately been unspecified.

REINVENTING YOURSELF AT ANY AGE

A Practical and Spiritual Instruction (Wo)manual

BY
TRUDY R. TOBIAS

"This is perhaps my biggest reinvention: Being at peace and knowing that no one can take that away from me."

~Trudy Tobias

"I love this book! It's loaded with style, just the right amount of cheekiness and hard-earned wisdom. I wish Trudy Tobias' professional insights and personal experience had been there following my divorce; it would have saved me a whole lot of time and heartache. I think it's the perfect book for any woman wondering how to reinvent or rediscover herself in midlife and beyond."

~Lina Landess, Author of '*Heart Breaking Open, Discovering the Heart Within Heartbreak*'

DEDICATION

This book is dedicated to the real Ilene, as well as the many other women with whom I have had the privilege of working, and hopefully, making a difference on their journey to reinventing themselves and living their truEST* lives.

*True Essential-Self Transformed

TABLE OF CONTENTS

"However I look and sound, whatever I say and do, and whatever I think and feel at a given moment in time is authentically me. If later some parts of how I looked, sounded, thought, and felt turn out to be unfitting, I can discard that which is unfitting, keep the rest, and invent something new for that which I discarded...I own me and therefore I can engineer me."

~Virginia Satir,
Pioneering Psychotherapist,
Lecturer, and Author

INTRODUCTION: ILENE, A REINVENTED WOMAN

"Life isn't about finding yourself. Life is about creating yourself."
~Author Unknown

It is 2:00 AM. Ilene turns over and awakens with a start. For a brief moment, she forgets what has awakened her. Then the all too familiar feelings of grief and panic sweep over her. Her beloved Darryl is gone. How could he have died? He wasn't supposed to go so soon. She should have stopped him from having that stupid operation. She knew it, she knew it. She knew it! Ilene starts sobbing. What was she ever going to do now that Darryl was gone? Hadn't she told him, just a moment before he complained of not feeling well, that she couldn't live without him? Whatever was she going to do now?

Ilene was 67 when Darryl, her beloved husband of 30 years, unexpectedly died of a heart attack. Darryl had just been discharged from the hospital after having had a successful stent procedure. Rather than drive home from the hospital which was 50 miles away from their home, Ilene and Darryl had decided to spend the night in a nice hotel three miles from the hospital. Ilene and Darryl were so happy that the procedure was behind them and were looking forward to a nice dinner brought up by room service. Ilene had just told Darryl "I couldn't live my life without you," when Darryl said he didn't feel well. The paramedics were called, but it was too late. Within three minutes, he was dead. Now this would have been a traumatic event for anyone. But for Ilene, her statement of "I couldn't live without you," was all too true. She had no life outside of Darryl.

This had been a second marriage for both Darryl and Ilene
never had children, and when they met, Darryl's 12 year c
living with his biological mom in her native Canada, so
Ilene were able to just focus on one another. While origi
was not particularly successful financially, after marryi
went up the corporate ladder very quickly. Ilene continue
a secretary and moved into an office manager position. Al
was friendly with the women with whom she worked, she d
out their friendship after working hours. Nonetheless, she enj
work and for the first time in her life, felt fairly competent. How
after fifteen years in a crowded area near Los Angeles, Da
convinced Ilene to move to a smaller city that was further south a
away from all the places and people Ilene knew.

At this time, Darryl retired from his corporate business and started hi
own business in real estate. Ilene went to work for Darryl, and she helped him run his business out of their home. Besides taking care of Darryl and becoming an immaculate, if not obsessive, housekeeper, Ilene had no outside interests. She didn't play golf, although they lived on a golf course, for Pete's sake! She wasn't a tennis lady either. Ilene and Darryl belonged to The Club only in order to go to its restaurant. Because Ilene wouldn't drive by herself more than thirty minutes just to do errands, and never traveled to visit family or her former friends without Darryl, her friendships from her former life drifted away and she had made no new friends in the area, preferring to just be with Darryl. Ilene's sister lived with a man whom Ilene didn't like, about two hours away and Ilene would have had to transverse the wonderful California freeway (perhaps parking lot is more accurate) between them, so she didn't see her sister unless Darryl drove her.

ıes, Ilene would express sadness and discontent to Darryl, crying o apparent reason. She could not account for her morose, and ɛr fully explored it. She convinced herself that she and Darryl were sfully happy in the beautiful home that they had created, and with e business and pleasure trips that they took. After living out in the naller community for about eight years, Darryl began experiencing ome health issues. He slowed down a lot and became reluctant to travel far. After feeling particularly tired for some time, Darryl had an ultrasound which revealed 90% heart blockage. Thus he had that operation and experienced that fateful and fatal heart attack.

Naturally, Ilene experienced deep and profound grief about Darryl's death. Ilene did get help with her grief by going to therapy and joining a widow's group, thereby getting some relief for the intense grief she was feeling. But it was not only grief that Ilene was experiencing. Ilene had become so dependent on Darryl that she didn't know how to manage by herself. She hated staying at home, but also had no one with whom to go out. Ilene felt distraught not only because of missing her husband, but also because she felt her life had no meaning or purpose. She was also filled with anxiety about what the future held even though Darryl had left her well off financially. She truly felt that she had no life now that her husband was gone.

Four months after Darryl's death, and Ilene was still waking up at 2 in the morning, full of anxiety. Her thoughts kept going around in circles: "Something must be wrong with me, I don't know how I can survive without Darryl, I have no life without him, I've never been alone before. I can't sleep, I can't eat, I can't concentrate enough to read anything. I have no hobbies. I've never gone anywhere without him. How will I survive? How am I going to get through this night? Tomorrow will be just as horrible. How will I get through the day? I have no friends here. How would I even make friends at my age? They probably wouldn't like me, anyhow. The people in this God forsaken place are just not my kind of folks. Maybe I should move closer to my sister, but I don't like the guy she's living with, and her daughter just got married and will be having kids any minute, and my sister works full time anyhow, so she has no time for me; and the friends I used to have probably have forgotten all about me, and I just want my Darryl back. He shouldn't have died! What am I going to do without him? How can I take care of the business he left me? I know his friend, Martin, is helping me, but I don't know a friggin' thing about the business. Darryl had tried to show me what to do, but I kept brushing him off. I just don't get it. How can I be so dumb? I hate my life, I hate it, I hate it, I hate it!"

Although logically Ilene knew that she was in good shape financially, emotionally she didn't believe it, and had to be constantly reassured by her husband's business manager/friend, Martin, that she was alright financially. While luckily finances were not the issue, and Ilene didn't have to work, she obsessed about how her skills were outdated and she probably couldn't get a job anyway. She didn't know what to do with herself or literally how to be. After she was over the most intense part of her grief, for which the therapy had helped, Ilene began to work with me to coach her on how "to get a life" – in her own words.

Ilene was following one of the two basic motivating factors for human behavior: we either move toward pleasure or away from pain, with the latter being the stronger. In Ilene's case, she didn't believe she would ever have pleasure again, but she knew she had to stop being in so much pain.

She knew she had to reinvent herself, whether or not she wanted to. She was no longer a wife, and knew she had to come up with another way of being. Her motivating factor was believing that if she couldn't create a new life for herself,

Darryl would be so disappointed in her after he had worked so hard at giving her a good life.

Ilene, like many of us, did not realize how strong she was until she knew that being strong was the only choice she had. While still missing her husband deeply, and having some days where the grief just hits her like a ton of bricks, Ilene has reinvented herself. As a matter of fact, as of this writing she is in Cabo San Lucas, Mexico, with a friend. Earlier in the year she flew by herself for the first time ever in her entire life to meet me in person. She has driven the two-hour plus to visit her sister and drove to visit a former roommate who lives even further away. Ilene now has peeps in her community to go out with to eat, to go to wine tastings, to shop and to celebrate her birthday or honor the passing of her husband. She has decided to stay in her home for now, and has someone who is helping her with her husband's business. She is on a bowling league, and plays bocce ball and Canasta. Ilene is also trying to find a place where she can volunteer. She recently told me that she would have gladly paid any amount of money to know that without Darryl she could still have a life that was worth living. She has realized that she doesn't need a man to define her, and that she does have a good life to enjoy.

Ilene is now living her truEST* life. As the saying goes "You've come a long way, baby!" She did it, I did it, countless people with whom I've worked, as well as friends, have done it and I know you can, too. If you want additional help in reinventing yourself after reading this book, I hope you will give me the honor of supporting you along the way to your truEST life, just as I did with Ilene.

If so, please contact me at;
Trudy@truestlifecoaching.com,
Trudy@truestlifecounseling.com,
or 336-763-4611.

*True Essential-Self Transformed

CHAPTER 1:
YOUR JOURNEY TO PICKING UP THIS (WO)MANUAL

"This is a test to see if your mission in this life is complete, if you are alive, it isn't."

~Richard Bach,
Illusions: The Adventures of a Reluctant Messiah

So now it's time to consider what has happened in your life that has drawn you to this (Wo)manual. (Pause, dear reader, and answer for yourself.) I assume that "reinventing yourself at any age" resonated with you in some way. What is that reason? (Again, pause and ask yourself.) And most importantly, since we human beings resist change, and change isn't easy, ask yourself, "Why do I want to reinvent myself?" As you will see later on, your Why is critical to the process.

Maybe your husband hasn't unexpectedly passed away, like Ilene's did. Maybe you're thinking about ending your marriage after years of frustration and sadness, as I did. Maybe it wasn't a shitty husband, but a shitty job. You're 50, 60, 70, whatever. And life (spelled S H I f T) has just happened. (That's my acronym for shit happens, something big has changed (shifted) and the world as you have known it has ended.) For whatever reason, by circumstances or by choice, you find yourself in uncharted waters. Anxiety about the future is swamping your boat and you're not sure if you can keep it afloat. I know anxiety and fear about the future can keep you, as it did me, stuck in the quagmire, whether it's an abusive relationship with a spouse or a boss, feeling that you are just too old to change, or whatever. But here you are, wondering "Who the hell am I? How the hell did I get here? And not having a damn clue what to do about it.

C'mon – take my "hand" as I lead you through my journey and yours to your TruEST Life, because...

"It's never too late to live happily ever after."

First, however, you also might be wondering, what does "reinvent yourself" actually mean? So let's start there. Since to invent means to create, discover, conceive, design, develop, dream up or conjure, it follows that to reinvent yourself means to create or design, develop or dream up some new way of being. Implicit in the definition is that there is hope for something better. Perhaps you find yourself in circumstances that require you to be different, such as what happened to Ilene. Sometimes you may be so unhappy with the way things are that you just want to start over again, such as you'll see in my story. Sometimes it can be a simple (not necessarily easy) thing, as deciding to stand up for yourself with your over-bearing co-worker, or it could mean moving across the country. Whatever the impetus, you may find that you need to reinvent yourself in order to follow your truEST life. When you are true to your essential self, you are honoring your Higher Self, your spirit, your soul, if you will – that part of you that is most closely connected to Source/Universe/ God. It is that part of you that is eternal, that came to Earth School for a purpose. When you are following your truEST life path, your purpose becomes clearer. You feel joyful, as if lit up from the inside; you feel your energy flow as your spirit lightens up. It means being you without needing or wanting anyone else's permission. This is not being selfish, but rather caring for yourself and who you are meant to be on your life's journey. (How are you feeling as you read those last couple of statements? Notice if you are anxious/scared, or anxious/excited and hopeful.)

Traditionally, this is a difficult concept, especially for women. As women, we are conditioned to be caretakers and nurturers, which accounts for why so many women are drawn to the helping professions, such as social work, nursing or teaching; it somewhat makes sense that women often give up themselves to help others. In addition, women traditionally define themselves by their relationships; who they are in context with another person, such as defining themselves as a wife or a mother. When that context changes, for example losing a spouse or having children leave home, women may not have a clue as to who they are. Especially after fifty, it seems that women often find themselves in uncharted waters – sometimes by choice, sometimes by circumstances. While Ilene did not make a conscious decision to change her life and was more or less forced into the necessity of recreating her life by an unwanted change of circumstances, there are many of us, myself included, who have chosen to finally make a change after years and years of resistance. We resist that still, small voice that is urging us to grow, because, let's face it, change is scary. Change, even change that we ask for, is scary. Anxiety about the future can run amok. We're scared to go out of our comfort zone, even if the zone is quicksand. It's often what has kept us stuck in our quagmire, whether it's an abusive relationship with a spouse or a boss. We confabulate – a great term in psychology – which means we make up stories to explain or justify our actions, and consequently stay in our discomfort. We rationalize that it's better to not rock the boat, to keep things the same because it would upset the applecart, meaning our children, our parents, our boss, our spouse/partner/ significant other or our dog. After all, as women we are conditioned to be people-pleasers. (Does any of this sound familiar?)

We think it's our job to make sure that everyone else has enough to eat before we partake a single morsel. It's our job to pour the oil on troubled waters; in fact, we are the oil! And it's no wonder that we feel all used up by the time we get to be 50+. We forget that we can't give others what we don't already have, that we can't pour water (or oil) from an empty cup, and that, as the airlines' flight attendants tell their customers, we must "Put your oxygen mask on first before helping others." Maybe it takes 50 plus years before our well is finally dry; maybe it takes that long to realize we can't confabulate any longer; maybe it takes that long to face our fears (**f**alse **e**vidence **a**ppearing **r**eal); maybe it takes that long, with what seems like the hour glass running faster, to decide that we deserve to be happy.

Whatever the reason, something seems to happen after fifty.

We start to listen, truly listen, to that little voice inside of us, you know, the one that's often called "Women's Intuition," which is actually our spirit/higher self/God/Universe, whatever fits for you, whispering to us to 'grow." More and more, women over fifty are realizing that it's time to listen to that voice. When we choose to ignore it, dire things can happen. When we choose to follow it, we start to reinvent ourselves and our lives.

CHAPTER 2: WHY REINVENT YOURSELF

"Growth is painful. Change is painful. But in the end, nothing is as painful as staying stuck somewhere you do not belong."

~Mandy Hale

It doesn't matter whether your need to reinvent yourself has come from something unexpected, like the death of a husband, like Ilene; it doesn't matter whether you choose the change, as I did; or have decided to move to a new community, or are retiring, or have kids going off to college. It doesn't matter what is prompting you to want to reinvent yourself. It doesn't matter what age you are, 50, 60, 70, or 80+. It doesn't matter what education you have or haven't had. It doesn't matter whether you are scrambling to pay your rent, or if you are as financially well off as Ilene. I understand you have doubts… you might be thinking that while it may be possible for others, you just are not sure if it's possible for YOU – that your situation is so unique or that you are such a mess or that you are so confused, you have no idea what it would mean to reinvent yourself or what the hell your truEST life could possibly be. However, the fact that you are still reading these words indicates to me that you have at least a little part of you that believes it is possible for you; you're hopeful or you wouldn't still be here. Let me assure you, as long as you have a mind, brain, and body, you will be able to do this! But first, you need to find your Why. (Remember me saying in Chapter 1 that it was critical to do so?)

For Ilene, it took her husband's passing to compel her to get out of her own way. I have to give her a lot of credit because she realized that unless she forced herself to get out of her comfort zone by feeling the fear and doing it anyway, she would have no life. She also felt she would be disappointing Darryl if she gave up, and the guilt she would experience was more painful for her than leaving her comfort zone. These, then, were her "Whys." They caused her to reinvent herself, to create a different life and an actual change of identity. Previously, Ilene had been a contented wife who relied on her husband to take care of her financially, physically and emotionally. She could no longer do that. She was forced to change – the whole time telling me that she didn't want to! It took a friend's death for me to have a strong enough Why or Desire to leave a marriage that was detrimental to me. I needed that Why to be strong – especially because I knew my daughter would be upset. For another client, Janice, it took getting fired from a job she detested before she had the courage to change not only her job but a long career in the non-profit world which was no longer feeding her soul.

Likewise, your Why has to be strong enough to endure the pain of change. I can't tell you when the scariness and fear over risking a new life and way of being will outweigh the pain of continuing to be stuck and unhappy. Each of us has a different pain threshold. After all, some of us choose natural childbirth and some of us can't or don't want to! We change only when the pain of staying stuck is stronger than the pain of venturing into the unknown. I have a beautiful painting in my office of a lovely ocean beach, with the words," You can't sail across the ocean until you have the courage to lose sight of the shore" which expresses these sentiments so poetically.

"The straw that breaks the camel's back" so to speak, is different for all of us. We may feel a longing or a discontent, which, according to Mary Morrissey, creator of the Dreambuilder® Program, are the two signs from the Universe whispering for us to grow. But those whispers may have to become shouts before you decide to take action, like it did for Janice by getting fired. If the catalyst for change lies within your conscious control, such as making a decision to change a job, relationship or a place to call home, it may be difficult to know what and when to do it. How will you know when the pain is enough for you? When it just is. When you feel like you have no choice. When you can't bear another moment of continuing down the path you are currently on. It may manifest itself in depression, weight gain or loss, panic attacks, headaches, or a myriad of ways, but there will be signs. Here's a question to ask yourself: "What would it be like for me to be in this same situation, to be feeling the same way I do now, a year from now? Five years from now?" If the notion just punches you in the gut, it may make sense to make the change now. If you do nothing, that is still making a choice. Whether you make a decision or not, 365 days are still going to pass in a year; 1,825 days will still pass in five years. Making a big life change is pretty scary, but don't let the concept of change scare you more than the prospect of remaining unhappy. Trust me, having regret is even scarier.

"Remember, you are only one decision away from a totally different life."

~Author Unknown

Therefore, dear reader, you can either read this book, decide that the concepts are interesting, and put it back on the "shelf," so to speak, or you can decide to read it, study it, do the exercises, and practice the changes and implement them in order to live your truEST life. It is my hope that the exercises and explanations involved here will give you the desire, the hope, the courage, and the belief that you can reinvent yourself, as well as the strategies to make that happen!

You deserve more in life. Let me assure you…it's really not too late for you. It wasn't too late for Ilene, and as you will see, it sure wasn't for me. You may just find out you have more strength than you ever thought possible. I know I did…hope you enjoy learning my story.

CHAPTER 3:
MY STORY: ANOTHER REINVENTED WOMAN

"So many people live within unhappy circumstances and yet will not take the initiative to change their situation because they are conditioned to a life of security, conformity, and conservation, all of which may appear to give one peace of mind, but in reality, nothing is more damaging to the adventurous spirit."

~Christopher McCandless

I had been unhappy in my marriage for years. Perhaps you can relate to that experience, or a similar one of being "stuck," or thinking that you were. I remember, when our daughter was two, sitting in a therapist's office and crying over my decision that although unhappy, I would stay in the marriage until my daughter was out of high school. I was sobbing at the realization that I was "in prison" for 16 more years. It seemed like a lifetime – and indeed it was. At that time in my life I was great at confabulating. (I do like that word!) I had decided that I would stay because my daughter had been adopted into our family, and I didn't want her to "lose" another family. I also didn't want her to have to go back and forth between homes. Since it had taken me so long to become a mom, just four months shy of 40 (we had tried for 10 years to have a child which resulted in one miscarriage and one premature infant who died six days after birth) that the thought of having my daughter not be with me while visiting her dad was more repugnant to me than staying in the marriage. I also thought about the finances (as a social worker in a non-profit, my salary wasn't stellar to say the least), and I also harbored the hope that things would get better.

I had met my second husband, Ray, in 1976. We had met when he was teaching the first self-improvement spiritual class I had ever attended, which was the impetus for the start of my spiritual journey. At the time I was still married to my first husband, Rick, who was as opposite to Ray as anyone could be. To quote my mother, "The only thing Rick and Ray have in common is a name starting with "R" and a penis!" In retrospect, I believe I married my first husband, Rick, because he was Jewish, which would please my parents. Although I am Jewish, Rick was the first Jewish guy I had dated in eight years. Needless to say, my parents weren't too happy about my previous boyfriends. Rick and I had known each other in grammar school and high school through mutual friends, but had never dated. We literally bumped into one another a year after college graduation, and Rick invited me to a party he was having. I thought it would be fun to see the friends we had in common, and came to the party with a date (my then long-distance boyfriend from college) so imagine my surprise when a few days after the party Rick called to ask me out. We had a really fun time over that summer, but I figured since Rick liked to have a good time and I had decided to go to grad school in the fall to get my Masters in Social Work degree, Rick would probably want to dump me since I wouldn't be available to "party" any more. To my surprise, he proposed instead. (One of my first lessons of the problems that could ensue in not listening to my inner guidance.) But my parents seemed to approve of him, we came from the same town, and it should work out, right? Actually three days before our wedding, I had a strong feeling that I shouldn't marry him, but I thought about the money my parents had already put out, how disappointed my parents would be, and about the people who were already in town for the wedding, and pushed those thoughts aside. (Second big lesson in not listening to my inner self.) Also, it's such a clear example of putting other people's needs before our own, isn't it? By the way, does putting other people's needs in front of your own sound familiar? I think recognizing the importance of, and acting upon creating self-care might be the most important part of reinventing oneself. (More on how healthy self-care is not the same as selfishness later.) So Rick and I married, and for the first two years it was okay. We never discussed having children, and frankly, I didn't want them with him (at least I listened to my inner guidance about that topic even though many of our friends, ones who had even gotten married after us, were starting their families; for once, I wasn't feeling pressured by what others thought). I divorced Rick because of his growing involvement with drugs, and his increasing capacity to lie. (I guess lying increasingly made sense when I found out after we had separated that he had been cheating on me - Lesson #3 in not listening to one's gut because the signs were all there!)

I do believe that my unhappiness in my first marriage is what led me to take the self-improvement spiritual class in which I met my second husband, Ray. It was touted to help relieve headaches (I was getting migraines at the time) and to develop one's intuition, among other things. I was already aware that I seemed to have intuitive abilities (although obviously I didn't always listen to them!) because I often thought of someone whom I hadn't heard from or seen in a long time, sometimes years – and they would get in touch with me that day or the next. In fact, one time I was talking on the phone to a grammar school friend, Hillary, and mentioned that I had not heard from one of our mutual friends, Ellen, in a couple of years, when literally the phone rang while the receiver was still in my hand from hanging up with Hillary, and it was, you guessed it – Ellen! Anyhow, you could see why I was attracted to this class (which used to be called Silva Mind Control; I believe the name has been changed to The Silva Method of

Mind Development, but it doesn't seem to be very active in the States now.) Anyhow, Ray and I had become friendly during the class, as well as afterwards because my girlfriend who went to the class with me coincidentally lived in the same apartment building as Ray. When visiting my friend, we would invite Ray to go out with us from time to time. It was several months (and a divorce) later that Ray and I were invited separately to this girlfriend's wedding, who, ironically enough, is still happily married to the man she had met in the exact same class! It was at that wedding that Ray's and my friendship began to develop into something more.

Although after a year of dating, I became aware while meditating, that I was scared Ray would propose and I wasn't ready yet, by the time he asked me six months later, I didn't give it another thought. I still wonder why I had no trepidations about marrying him like I had with Rick. Maybe it was because I hadn't listened to my intuition before, or maybe there were life lessons I had to learn from being with Ray, or because we had set up some type of agreement in a previous life (if that's a little woo woo for you, I understand.) Now this time my parents weren't too pleased because, you guessed it, Ray isn't Jewish. Nevertheless, "our song" was Debbie Boone's "You Light Up My Life." There was one stanza in there, "It can't be wrong if it feels so right..." which at the time captured what I felt.

Anyhow, back to my mom's comment about the only similarity between Rick and Ray was having a penis (have to put in an aside here – while proof-reading this, I noticed I had written "was ***being*** a penis" – don't you just love Freudian slips?): Rick – Jewish; Ray – not only Catholic but had been in the Christian Brothers before deciding he didn't want to give up women (in case you are as uninformed as I was,

Christian Brothers is a Catholic teaching order in which the Brothers take the same vows as priests do, except they can't perform any sacraments like marriage or last rites). Rick – dark hair, brown eyes, short and broad; Ray – tall, lean, blondish hair and blue eyes. Rick – party guy, spend-thrift, lots of friends, and into drugs; Ray – as straight as could be and worked seven days a week – five teaching in a Catholic school and teaching the Silva course every weekend, few friends, extremely frugal. Rick – sloppy; Ray – compulsively neat; Rick – a liar and cheat; Ray – told me he wouldn't have ever dated me if I had come onto him while still married to Rick. Rick – never discussed children; Ray – asked me if I wanted children on our third date. You get the idea.

So what went wrong with my marriage to Ray? Perhaps I chose him because he was so opposite of Rick in every way, but I like to think I was attracted to him because he was on a spiritual path as I was. Unfortunately, life (otherwise known as SHIfT) happened. Because we were older when we married, 30 for me, 38 for Ray, three months after marriage we started trying to have a family. We had no obvious or apparent reasons for our inability to conceive, but after two years we began the arduous journey of infertility treatment. It turns out we both were contributors to the lack of success in that department. People would often say, "Well, at least you're having fun trying." Trust me, it is not the least bit fun! It isn't fun to have to have relations because it's the right time of the month even though you had an argument a few hours before, and it isn't fun to refrain from intimacy when you're in the mood in order to build up sperm count. Infertility definitely takes a toll. Nevertheless, with the help of infertility drugs and interventions, I was eventually able to get pregnant – twice. The first pregnancy ended in miscarriage at eight weeks, and the second ended in a very premature birth of our son, Alex, who only lived for six days. Things went even further south when our son died since, at that same time,

Ray's teaching job – for the first time in a public school instead of a Catholic school – ended. This was probably Ray's favorite job; it was right near the house – in fact, it was the high school our daughter later attended – and he loved the curriculum and his colleagues. However, due to a lack of enrollment in his department, the position had changed to part-time, concurrent with the time we thought I would be on unpaid maternity leave. So I told Ray he needed to look for a full-time job, which both of us presumed he would easily find. After Alex died, neither of us were thinking straight for understandable reasons, so neither of us thought of Ray checking to see if he could work part-time at the school he had just left, since I was going back to work, after all. During the summer that our son died, the Silva business also moved out to California leaving Ray with no source of income. While I despondently went back to my school social work position, Ray was out of work for eight months before finding a job as a training instructor for the Illinois State Police, 50 miles from our home. Both Ray and I had thrown our spiritual beliefs out the window – we literally threw the baby out with the bath water (pun intended) at a time when we needed them most. When we were fortunate enough to adopt our daughter 18 months later, through many so-called coincidences (coincidences many say are actually the Universe/God performing miracles anonymously), I thought things between Ray and me would greatly improve and for a while, life seemed good again. (To be honest, if I could have divorced me after our son died, I would have; I was miserable as well as a miserable person to be around. I have to give Ray credit for hanging in there with a very depressed and angry partner.)

Nonetheless, Ray longed to be in the classroom again, and seemed to always be frustrated and angry because he wasn't. I naively thought if he could become a teacher again, this angry and out-of-sorts man who had replaced the one I had married, might leave, and the kinder, softer man who was spiritually inclined would return. For whatever reasons, that person never showed up (at least not to me) again. So I became more and more despondent and upset about the marriage and our relationship. In my truth (smaller case truth is Telling and Re-telling your Understanding of what you Think Happened) I felt controlled by and undermined by my husband, which I admit I allowed to happen in an effort to keep the peace as much as possible. (That had always been my role in my family of origin and I still played it well; I imagine it contributed to my choice to marry a "nice, Jewish man" the first time around as well. Again, you might want to stop here and think about if this is a role with which you can also identify.) I saw myself and believed myself to be a victim of his controlling actions, when all along I had the power to stop it if I had been more willing to risk confrontation.

Those are the reasons I found myself two years later in that therapist's office, ignoring my own needs, crying piteously, and deciding to stay in the "prison" of my own creation. I really wasn't trying to be a martyr. I had my reasons and justifications for staying. Whether that was the best choice for my daughter is still up for debate. Looking back, I know it cost me a great deal. I gained fifty pounds, pushing my emotions down and trying to keep them down. Not allowing myself to feel what I was feeling, I was figuratively and literally weighing myself down. But I had made my decision to stay in the marriage, and I was sticking with it, no matter the cost. Honestly, there's a part of me that was confounded by Me! After all, I'm fairly intelligent and have been a psycho-therapist for many years. I believe I have made a difference in my clients' lives for the better. Yet, here I was, making unsupportive and constricting decisions for my own life. If you hold onto the belief, as I did, that I must have everyone's approval all the time (see the chapter on Beliefs) then it's understandable that even with all the knowledge I had, I couldn't break out of my self-sabotaging habits. That is, until with the help of a good therapist, I began to realize that I deserved to be happy, and that I am worthwhile, even if it means others may not approve. While this was a good start, the magic key didn't happen for me until I re-instated my spiritual beliefs and practices when I moved to Greensboro, NC. Indeed, moving to North Carolina helped me find my true *North*.

For a variety of conscious reasons, when our daughter was 18, Ray and I thought it would be best to move away from the Chicago area. For subconscious reasons (or perhaps that intuitive part of me) I had been drawn to Greensboro, North Carolina, a community I had gotten to know when I visited a good friend of mine who had moved there fifteen years earlier. There was something about the "vibes" that made it feel like home to me. So when I needed a new job, I began to look for one in Greensboro, as well as in Chicago. During this time I had already started back on my spiritual path; therefore, I was very open to the idea that wherever I got a job was where I/we were supposed to be. I found and was hired for what I thought was my dream job in Greensboro, and was planning on it being the job from which I would retire. I had to move to NC to start the job before Ray and I had sold our house, so Ray stayed in Illinois until the deed (pun again intended) was done. It was during this period that I realized that I didn't miss him, and was managing well on my own, thank you very much. But how could I say that to Ray? He had no one and no reason to stay in Chicago (by this time he was out of work from yet another job), his parents who had lived in Indiana had passed away, and he still had only one or two people whom he considered to be friends. So again, I buckled up, or maybe it's buckled down, and didn't separate from Ray, putting someone else's needs in front of my own. Again, this may be familiar for you as well…just sayin'. Not only was I concerned about his feelings, but even more, my daughter's, who was/is definitely a Daddy's girl. Although she was now 18, I figured she would never forgive me if I left (which still might be the case). It took the passing of a dear friend of mine for me to look at my life, and to ask myself if this is how I wanted to live the rest of my life. The clear answer was "no."

This time I had support in listening to my gut; perhaps that was the real reason I had been drawn to Greensboro. As they say, God/the Universe works in mysterious ways. Shortly after moving to Greensboro, I joined a wonderful spiritual community, Unity, which put me squarely back on my spiritual path. I met wonderful friends who supported me, and availed myself to the wisdom of a spiritual leader, plus an excellent therapist. The combination of counseling, coaching and spirituality is how I reinvented myself. With their help, I started rethinking long-held beliefs, such as needing everyone's approval, and that it was wrong – maybe even evil, but certainly – oh, no! – selfish to be true to my own self and needs. (Stop and ponder whether these thoughts and accompanying feelings are familiar for you.) With the help of Unity Truth principles, I realized I could still be loving and caring, as well as spiritual even while taking care of myself. I started re-thinking my own value and self-worth, and through the use of positive affirmations, reframed self-talk, creating new beliefs, and firmly understanding the importance of self-care (all of which you will learn in the following chapters), I was able to reinvent myself. I became someone who was able to stand up for herself, listen to her intuition and follow it, and reclaim herself without anyone else's approval except her own.

So I stand before you now as someone who moved to a different part of the country in her late fifties even though my family of origin was angry about it, chose to leave a marriage which was not spiritually or emotionally supportive even though my daughter and ex-husband were upset about it, and changed jobs not once but five times – all in my sixties! Other changes which have occurred are my daughter leaving home and moving to California where she has started her own family and has blessed me with three grandsons – yay – and, sadly, the passing of both of my parents. These latter changes certainly affected my self-identity, as well. Nonetheless, I couldn't be happier. I have lost the weight I put on, have a wonderful group of friends and colleagues, and am still close with my sister who lives in Chicago and her family. In the last year I retired from a dream therapy job that I greatly enjoyed and which offered so-called security, to start up two businesses, a private practice counseling business and a separate coaching business, designed for women like me; women who are older and hopefully wiser, but just don't know how to get out of their own way, to leave their comfort zone, to reinvent themselves, and to start their truEST life. I decided to go into business for myself so that I could still make a difference in people's lives while enjoying the time and money freedom to visit my daughter and my sister more often, plus have a few fun vacays along the way (like going on a Mediterranean cruise in a few months with my BFF for instance). Yes, my daughter is still struggling with the idea that her parents are no longer together, but I have learned to accept that and make peace with it by using the tools you will learn how to use here. This is perhaps my biggest reinvention – being at peace and knowing that no one can take that away from me unless I let them. After all, I'm almost 70 and it's time for me! Hopefully, as I teach you how to use these tools, you'll conclude that it's time for you, too! Let's get started!

CHAPTER 4: VISION, THE (WO)MANUAL INSTRUCTIONAL DIAGRAM TO FOLLOW

"Our deepest fear is not that we are inadequate. Our deepest fear is that we are powerful beyond measure. It is our light, not our darkness that most frightens us."

~Marianne Williamson

What would your world be like, what would *you* be like, if you let your light shine? What if instead of being a victim you became a victor? What would it be like if you reinvented yourself and led your truEST life? If you're saying "I have NO idea, I'm confused and messed up. I don't know of another way to be or to act! That's the reason I picked up this book, for Pete's sake!" I understand. Those thoughts are natural. I had them, too. Those thoughts and feelings are also designed to trick you and me into thinking that it's okay to play small. Being confused allows us to do nothing.

If you wanted to take a trip, say from where you live to somewhere else, how would you do it? First you'd say to me, "Are you crazy? What do you mean, 'somewhere?' I can't take a trip to *somewhere.* I'd have to know where I'm going. I'd have to have a destination." And that is exactly right. Of course you would. So let's say you choose a city where you have never been but have heard wonderful things about. You have always wanted to go there. Let's say it's New York City and you are excited about going. You want to eat the great food, see the amazing shows, and shop until you drop! So now you have your destination in mind. But you don't know *how* to get there. You need to decide whether to fly, take a train or a bus, or go by car. In the case of a plane, you would sure hope that the pilot knew what coordinates to set in order to fly from point A to New York. Likewise, you would rely on the train conductor to know which tracks to take, or the bus driver to know the route, even if you didn't. In the "olden days" if you yourself were driving, you would take out a map or several maps and plan your trip. Or you would go to AAA and get a TripTik. Nowadays, you get in your car and use Google Maps or your GPS to guide you. You don't have to know the how, which highways and byways to take. As long as you have your destination in mind, you just have to know what instrument to use to guide you there.

So the first instrument, your map, so to speak, in reinventing yourself and finding your truEST life is to create a vision of what you would really love to have and how you would love to be in your life. Don't look at what ***is*** for right now. Ignore the current conditions and so-called facts, especially the number of birthdays you have had, or what you think is logical. Instead, ask yourself, "If I could wave the proverbial magic wand, (let's think of it as the Possibility Wand), what would I love to have and what would I love to be in my life?" You don't have to know the How. The Universe will supply the way (the How), just as the GPS does. Only ask yourself, "What would I love to have and how would I like to be in my life?" That may seem overwhelming and you may think you don't know where to start, so let's break it down a bit. Since life is not one dimensional, in order to reinvent yourself and create a life you truly love, it is necessary to address several areas/domains/ categories.

Mary Morrissey says to ask yourself the question, "What would I love?" in four domains: Health and Well-Being, Relationships, Vocation or Vocare, and Time/Money Freedom, to create a life you would love. In his Virtual Coaching program, Eben Pagan uses the acronym BEMERI, which stands for areas that just involve yourself - Body, Emotions, Mind, and areas that you share with others - Environment, Relationships and Ideas, to envision what you would want in your life. The Silva Method teaches practices that focus on what you want Physically, Emotionally, Mentally, and Spiritually. James Arthur Ray in his book, Harmonic Wealth, uses five pillars to create a successful life: Financial, Relational. Mental, Physical, and Spiritual. Obviously, there are overlaps and variances in every system.

For now, let's combine these systems in the following ways: Health and Well-Being will consist of your body's physical, mental, emotional and spiritual health. Relationships will cover your relationships with a spouse, partner, or significant other, whether one is present in your life right now or you would like one to be. Relationships will also cover how you get along with other family members including parents, siblings, children, cousins, etc. People whom you consider to be friends, work colleagues, parishioners from your house of worship, or neighbors would also fall under the Relationships category. Most importantly, the relationship you have with yourself, including a sense of self-worth is in this category while also being a part of the Health and Well-Being dimension since mental and emotional health are interdependent with our sense of self-worth, (I will discuss this more in depth later.) Vocation/Vocare covers your work and/or hobbies; whatever you like to do with or without pay. James Arthur Ray's financial pillar for success is part of this category. Ask yourself, "How do I want to spend my time?" Morrissey's Time/Money Freedom comes to play here because I would imagine in your ideal world you would want to enjoy what you are doing inside and outside of your occupation. Eben Pagan's Environment category is the category in which you ask yourself such questions as "Where do I like spending my time?" and when there, "How do I like my space to be?" For example, you may love being at home as long as it is clean and neat but not so much if it looks like a tornado just went through it. There's also an overlap with Rela-tion-ships here, such as asking "Who do I want to have in my Environment?"

Come up with one answer in each category. To rewire your brain in order to imagine and believe your vision, here's what to do:

- Create the answers with statements using the present tense, in the here and now, instead of the future (It's the difference between saying I will weigh my ideal weight, and I weigh my ideal weight. Which seems to have more power to manifest?)
- State your answers positively, focusing on what you want instead of what you don't want (i.e. "I am healthy" instead of "I am not sick.") because our brains can't process a negative command (more on how our brains work in a later chapter.)
- Use "I am" statements as much as possible because there is a law in psychology that whatever is attached to the "I am" – as long as there is enough Desire, Belief and Expectancy – comes into fruition.
- Add gratitude to all that you have in your vision to raise the vibrations and allow the manifestation to come forth. Sometimes my clients have difficulty being grateful for what has not yet occurred or manifested on the physical plane. However, as the great Way-Shower, Jesus, demonstrated when he thanked God before the mana and fish appeared, or before a healing occurred, or before Lazarus rose from the dead, being grateful validates faith (Belief) that what is desired has already been created.

VISION TOOL:

If you would like some help in creating your vision, you can use the following as a template:

Physically, I am healthy with a strong immune system, and

____

____

____

Thank you, God. (or Universe or Great Spirit, whatever works for you.)

Emotionally, I am stable and

____

____

____

Thank you, God. (or Universe or Great Spirit, whatever works for you.)

Mentally, I have a positive outlook and

____

____

____

Thank you, God. (or Universe or Great Spirit, whatever works for you.)

Spiritually, I am growing in the virtues of faith, intuition, hope and love

____

____

____

Thank you, God. (or Universe or Great Spirit, whatever works for you.)

I am enjoying my relationship(s) with

____

____

____

I am loving these relationships because they are uplifting and supportive and

____

____

____

Thank you, God. (or Universe or Great Spirit, whatever works for you.)

I am enjoying and loving my relationship with myself. I know I am worthy and

____

____

____

Thank you, God. (or Universe or Great Spirit, whatever works for you.)

I am enjoying the work that I do. I am now

____

____

____

____

____

Thank you, God. (or Universe or Great Spirit, whatever works for you.)

I am loving how my work helps me serve the world by

____

____

____

____

____

Thank you, God. (or Universe or Great Spirit, whatever works for you.)

I am fulfilled by my hobbies and interests, and love having the time and money to do them. I am having so much fun with/by doing

____

____

____

____

____

Thank you, God. (or Universe or Great Spirit, whatever works for you.)

I am earning $__________ (be specific here) annually. I am loving the time and money freedom that earning this income affords me. As a result of this income, I am now able to spend my time

____

____

____

____

Thank you, God. (or Universe or Great Spirit, whatever works for you.)

I am enjoying the environment I have created at work and at home. I am loving that my space is

____

____

____

____

Thank you, God. (or Universe or Great Spirit, whatever works for you.)

For all of these things, or for something better, I am truly grateful. Thank you, thank you, thank you!

(Make copies of Appendix A)

To help you further with this process, here is an example of the vision that I used to reinvent myself to live my truEST life:

Physically, I am healthy with a strong immune system. I am full of energy, vitality, and zeal. I am loving my body and taking good care of it. I am so happy with the strength and flexibility I now have. I am maintaining my ideal weight of 148 with ease.

Thank you, God.

Emotionally, I am stable and loving that I am so balanced. I am allowing myself to feel all of my feelings with peace and grace.

Thank you, God.

Mentally, I have a positive outlook and I am able to keep my focus on thoughts that are for my highest good.

Thank you, God.

Spiritually, I am growing in the virtues of faith, intuition, hope and love. I am trusting my higher self more each day.

Thank you, God.

I am enjoying my relationship with my daughter. I am authentic and truthful with her as she is with me. I am respectful of her opinions and I am allowing her to express them freely. I am so happy that she and I are enjoying the closest relationship that we have ever had.

I am filled with joy and love with the relationships I have with my friends and family, both near and far. I am connected with so many people, for which I am truly grateful. I am loving these uplifting and supportive relationships.

I am enjoying a supportive and loving relationship with a wonderful man who appreciates me for me. I am so happy that we share our love of animals, and that we are both seeking to evolve spiritually.**

Thank you, God.

I am enjoying and loving my relationship with myself. I know I am worthy and deserving to have and to be everything that I desire. I love the caring, loving, considerate, fun, happy person that I am.

Thank you, God.

I am enjoying the work that I do. I am now a private mental health practitioner and I am also a Transitions Life Coach serving the ideal number of terrific clients. I am loving how my work helps me serve the world by helping women like me who are re-creating themselves and their lives so that they can also live lives that they love and truly deserve.

Thank you, God.

I am fulfilled by my hobbies and interests. I am having so much fun working out and getting stronger each day as a result – taking Zumba classes, painting, doing needlepoint, writing, and traveling in my camper with my pets.

Thank you, God.

I am earning $200,000.00 annually. I am loving the time and money freedom that earning this income affords me. I am now spending my time seeing my daughter and her family in California at least four times a year, seeing my sister and her family in Chicago and in Florida, three times a year or more, and seeing at least one good friend who lives in another state annually. I am enjoying one special trip a year and am so happy to be going to the Mediterranean this year.

Thank you, God.

I am enjoying the environment I have created at work and at home. I love my house and how it reflects my inner being and raises my spirits. I am loving that I am able to work out of my house and that I can also work when I travel. I love the office I have created in my home and that it is a welcoming environment for clients.

Thank you, God.

For all of these things, or for something better, I am truly grateful. Thank you, God, thank you, thank you!

** While this relationship has not yet manifested in the world, I remain happy and grateful for its creation.

Another popular exercise to help you with your vision is to create a Vision Board, also known as Treasure Mapping. Again, in the olden days, folks would tear pictures and words out of magazines to glue onto a poster board to create their Vision Board. Thanks to the Internet, you can just use Google Images to search for quotes or pictures of whatever you want, and then scroll through your options. Whatever resonates with you is what is appealing to your higher or intuitive essential self. Print those puppies out and post on a board, or there are now programs that are entirely electronic. Because the human brain thinks in pictures, having something visual to look at reinforces and focuses the vision of what we want in our lives in order for the Universe/God/Higher Selves/Source to bring those things into manifestation. Some experts in Treasure Mapping, such as Jane Alexander, recommend that you just focus on one area of your life at a time. However, since we are talking about reinventing yourself to live your truEST life, and life is multi-dimensional, I personally like using a gestalt of the life you are in the midst of creating. Sometimes arranging the pictures in categories can help you organize what you want. Here is a photo of my vision board to illustrate how a vision board might be helpful to you. As I hope you can see, I used the four domains that Mary Morrissey recommends, and have posted pictures and sayings of what I want using the four corners of the board to reflect each of the four domains.

However, just completing the answer template or creating a Vision Board is not enough to bring your desires into manifestation. The most important thing about creating a Vision Board or Vision

Statements is to envision, that is to enter the vision as if it were already true. Think and feel your vision to be an energy field that surrounds you. This field of energy permeates your body, mind, spirit, and every aspect of your life in physicality. As you feel this energy, you begin to live and to behave as though your vision has already been realized. Your current actions, not just your list of goals, then come *from* the vision. You are then able to integrate all aspects of your life to create your truEST life, thereby reinventing yourself from the inside out. For example, in my vision I am a person who maintains my ideal weight easily, and as someone who is this way, I no longer have to struggle with whether or not to have that piece of chocolate cake. It no longer fits the vision of who I am. Since in my vision I am a person who is emotionally balanced, I now respond rather than react to life circumstances, thereby enriching all of my relationships.

According to Susan Walsh of Unprecedented Lives®, "Where many people fail to bring their vision into reality is that they dream up a life they'd love, maybe even write it down, but then don't relate to it as already being that person who has it. How would you behave as the person who is already living that dream life? What would your thoughts be...how would you be feeling, how would you relate to the world? If you want your vision to become your reality, you must first become that person in your vision." To help in this process, Mary Morrissey in her Life Mastery Program® has clients meditate daily upon their vision, and write daily how their life will be in six months. In addition, Morrissey has her clients write out daily for what and in what they are grateful, what they are creating that day, and what and how they are being that day by completing the sentence "I am..."

Now that you know your destination (Vision), let's get the GPS set for the first leg of your journey to your truEST life!

CHAPTER 5: SCHEMATIC FOR SELF-REINVENTION

"The starting point of all achievement is desire."

~Napoleon Hill

The first of the three parts to the schematic that you will need in reinventing yourself is Desire. Desire seems like it should be a no-brainer, but it really isn't. That's because there can be a part of you that wants to change; simultaneously, there can be a part of you that resists change. That's true for everyone because, as mentioned before, change is scary. Humans by nature prefer homeostasis – that is, we like things to stay the same. Staying the same is safe. It is our ego's job to keep us safe, and the ego will fight like hell to do just that. However, especially in today's techie world, we are living with the only constant being change. This can create a lot of friction within us which needs to be addressed. In a later chapter, you will find that, as the saying goes, "We have an app (technique) for that!" In the meantime, if you want to know whether your Desire for change is more powerful than your ego's desire for safety, just look at your life. Are you in the same situation you were in last week, last month, last year, the last five years? If so, that is a clue that you have had some unidentified thoughts and feelings that need to be brought into awareness for them to be changed. It's like wanting to reduce weight while simultaneously eating the chocolate cake – it can't effectively be done. It also reminds me of the story of the old Cherokee chief who was teaching his grandson about life. "A fight is going on inside me," the Chief said to the boy. "It is a terrible fight and it is between two wolves." ... "Which wolf will win?" asked the boy. The old chief simply replied, "The one I feed." This parable has been used a lot in different contexts to illustrate the "fight" between positive and negative thoughts, or between contradictory goals. It is also true of the conflict between wanting change (Desire) and resistance to change. It is our *attention* not our *intention* that rules the day. So please ask yourself, which wolf are you going to feed? Have no worries if your desire is not on fire right now; in the next chapter you will learn strategies to flame it!

"The only limits you have are the limits you believe."

~Wayne Dyer

Belief, with a capital B, as it is used in this context, stands for faith, and is the second part of the schematic. It is the belief that something not yet seen on the physical plane has already occurred or can occur. While the saying goes, "Seeing is believing" it is actually the other way around, "Believing is seeing." Belief is literally stepping out in faith. It's like in the Indiana Jones movie when Indy had to cross the invisible bridge. It was only by Indy stepping off the cliff (out in faith) that the bridge appeared. Staying with the movie theme, remember in the movie Apollo 13 when Ed Harris, who was playing the Flight Director, Eugene Francis "Gene" Kranz, stated, "Failure is not an option."?* Since it wasn't an option, the engineers literally figured out a way to put square pegs into round holes (or was it the other way around? – No matter – you get what I'm saying.)

*"Failure is not an option" was in fact coined by Bill Broyles, one of the screenwriters of Apollo 13, based on a similar statement made not by Kranz, but another member of the Apollo 13 mission control crew, FDO Flight Controller Jerry Bostick. According to Bostick, his statement actually was "... when bad things happened, we just calmly laid out all the options, and failure was not one of them."

It was the same for great inventors, such as Thomas Edison, Henry Ford, and the Wright Brothers, as well as outstanding athletes like Babe Ruth and Michael Jordan, who believed, or had faith, that they would succeed, and consequently, did not let any setbacks slow them down. Instead, they used the setbacks as feedback to know what would or wouldn't work. Therefore, Belief, as it is used here, is faith that something will occur, despite the facts or conditions that may be present on the physical plane. Doubt may lie (double entendre intended) before us. Nevertheless, I want you to promise yourself, here and now, that you will hold onto your belief that you can step out of your comfort zone and create a new life for yourself. When you feel doubt come up, hang onto my belief in you. I was able to do it, Ilene was able to do it, and so have the many other clients with whom I've had the privilege to work. Knowing that others have done it will hopefully help to strengthen your Belief. To illustrate how someone else doing what you want to do can affect your ability to believe that you can do it too, in 1954 Englishman Sir Roger Bannister rewrote the record books when he became the first person to run a mile in under four minutes. Up until then scientists had said it was impossible for the human body to run that fast. Luckily, Roger didn't give the scientific world much credence, and so he was able to run a sub-four-minute mile. Here's what's interesting – within a year of Bannister accomplishing that feat, 200 other men were also able to do it. Once runners believed it was possible, they could say to themselves, "If Sir Roger can do it, so can I." So if Ilene can do it, if I can do it, believe that you can do it, too!

"Faith is Expectancy. You do not receive what you want, you do not receive what you pray for, not even what you say you have faith in. You will always receive what you actually expect."

~Eric Butterworth

Expectancy, the third part of the schematic in our Instruction (Wo)manual for reinvention of self, is actually the visualization and feeling state of the Belief, as if the Belief has already manifested. All three are necessary instruments in reinventing ourselves. Doubt and anxiety can cut us off at the knees if we allow it. Those two demons can interfere with not only Belief and Expectancy, but can also begin to affect our Desire if we let them. And that is the key to success; we human beings have the ability to choose. We can decide what we want to focus on, no matter what circumstances, conditions, or "facts" appear. We don't deny the obstacles, but we deny allowing them to have power over us! We attend to only the vision we want to see and the feelings we want to have. It is our *attention* - not our *intention* - that matters.

Once we have these tools to use, we can then proceed to work with our Bio-Computer System, our Mind, Brain, and Body to get the results we seek. As far as I know, everyone has one of each, so anyone and everyone can make the changes to reinvent themselves. While I will discuss these more in depth in the next chapter, briefly, we can liken our Minds to being the programmer of our Bio-Computer System. Our brains are like the CPU of the computer itself. It can only do what it has been programmed to do. For example, if we brought a computer that had been programmed in Great Britain over to the U.S., it would indicate that the word, "behavior," is spelled "behaviour." As I type this, my American English programmed computer has indicated by the red squiggly line that behavio**u**r is indeed spelled incorrectly. Likewise, the King's English programmed computer would not be capable of realizing that it is now in America so it must act accordingly. It will have to be reprogrammed first. While our Minds can create a new program, our Brains can only do what they are programmed to do. To continue our Bio-Computer analogy, the body is the print-out from the computer. If our brains tell our bodies something, our bodies will gladly comply.

The fourth area on which we will work, which I have already indicated is the key for sustainable change, is the Spirit. This could be interpreted in a religious sense if you're comfortable with that notion, but if you are agnostic or atheist and are uncomfortable with the idea that there is a Spirit or Higher Self which indwells in everyone, you can just stick with the Mind and/or Intuition for now since they also exist in the spiritual (non-physical) realm. (I will say that if you can have Faith that there is a Higher Self already within you that already sees the best in you and is just waiting for you to allow it to shine, change will be easier.) Spirit and Mind exist in the non-physical realm because both the Spirit and the Mind are invisible to our naked human eyes. Although invisible, that doesn't mean that they don't exist. I mean, if our heads and bodies were suddenly invisible, could anyone see where our minds are? (Actually, I often wonder where mine is, especially when it's not attending to what my body is doing, as in, "Where did I put my keys?" but that's a whole other area for discussion.) Another example of being non-physical is that while we may change our minds, we haven't changed our brains - although that might not be too far off in the scientific/ medical/genetic world of the future.

What's crucial to realize about the Mind is that everything has to exist in Mind before it can exist in matter. Look around and you will see that is true. Everything that has ever been created has first existed in thought – even us! Whether planned or not, some creative force had to think of getting that sperm to that egg in order for us to exist in these skin bags, known as our bodies. It is by using our bodies that we are capable of taking action on our thoughts and beliefs. In our world, just thinking about something will not create it. We cannot sit on a mountaintop all day contemplating our navels and expect results on this earth plane without also taking action. So while Edison's, Ford's, and the Wright Brothers' faith was steadfast, they also had to create their inventions by taking action, trying out things until they actually worked. In addition, it is with our bodies that we feel our emotional states. Through our bodies we are able to identify those states, which fall into four basic categories: sad, mad, glad, and afraid. There are many nuances to these basic four, all of which must be identified on the Abraham Hicks Emotional Scale (see Chapter 8) in order to move up the emotional ladder and thereby change our vibrations. As we will see later on, the vibrations that emerge from our feelings either magnetize or repel the results that we want to manifest in our lives. If you're familiar with The Law of Attraction by Esther and Jerry Hicks, or the movie, "The Secret," you know of which I speak. Via these vibrations, we will learn how to draw what we want into our lives in order to live our truEST lives.

In sum, you need three tools to reinvent yourself or become your truEST self, living your truEST life: Desire or pure intention, with nothing that counters it ***for*** change to occur; Belief or Faith that change ***can*** occur, and Expectancy, or a clear positive vision with feelings that the desired vision/result ***has already*** occurred. The Instruction (Wo)manual calls for you to use these three tools to tinker with your Bio-Computer System, which is made up of your Mind, Brain, and Spirit to recreate your inner workings. Once your inner works have been successfully transformed, your outer world will have to reflect those changes and will manifest in your body and by your body through actions and feelings. And ta dah, one new reinvented you coming right up!

CHAPTER 6: STEP ONE: CHANGING THOUGHTS

While Desire, Belief and Expectancy are required to begin the process of reinventing yourself, the IT Department (you) also requires understanding how your mind, brain and body work together; how your thoughts and beliefs have created your life up until now, and how you can use strategies and tools to reinvent yourself and create a new life that you love by changing those thoughts and beliefs. The tools and strategies utilized in this book, and the more in-depth ones I use in my coaching, combine the best that I have used in my 44+ years as a licensed clinical social worker and as a transitions coach. More importantly, you'll learn exercises from my decades-long spiritual journey, which will increase your intuition and ability to follow your own path to your truEST life. For me, those exercises are the most important for transformation and reinventing your life.

"Your brain is a radio transmitter. It broadcasts thoughts, directions & vibrations to your cells. You choose the station it's tuned to."

~Kris Carr

Understanding How Your Brain Works:

I'm sure you'll agree, with maybe the exception of the Scarecrow in The Wizard of Oz, that we all have a brain. So, okay, assuming that you, dear reader, are not Oz's scarecrow, I think it's safe to say that you have a brain. I am going to go a bit into teacher mode to introduce some concepts about the mind, brain, body, and spirit so you will understand how they all work together. To reinvent yourself, you need to work on all four areas to create lasting change.

So, let's start with the brain. I would imagine that some of this you already know, but I want you to really understand how this relates to reinventing yourself for good (last word being used two ways!) Here are some interesting facts about our brains. Did you know that the average adult brain weighs about 2.5 pounds? That it takes in about 10,000 bits of info a second, more than any computer? The brain also has a left and right hemisphere. The Left hemisphere deals with Logic (easy to remember, L and L). It is that part of our brain which is like Mr. Spock or Data of Star Trek fame, always wanting to solve problems logically. However, if logic alone were sufficient to enjoy a full life, Mr. Spock and Data wouldn't have kept trying so hard to become human and to feel emotions, as messy as they sometimes can be. It is our right hemisphere that deals with those emotions, as well as intuition, imagination, and creativity. Our left brain hemisphere helps with math and sees each tree in the forest, while our right side sees the big picture or the forest. Both hemispheres are connected by the corpus callosum, which allows each hemisphere to talk back and forth with one another. I have designed this book and the exercises in it to appeal to both brain hemispheres. Your right brain hemisphere is happy to go along with the exercises, but unless the left side of your brain is satisfied that what is happening makes sense, it can sabotage their effectiveness.

In addition to understanding that we have two brain hemispheres that serve different functions, it's important to realize that down through the ages our brains have been hardwired based on fear. This makes sense when we realize that it was necessary for human survival. Let's face it – our species was not created with the ability to be very fast, or very strong, or to have sharp claws and teeth with which to defend ourselves. All we had were our brains to help us survive, so we still respond to danger, whether real or not, the same way the caveman did. We have a fight, flight, or freeze response to danger. As a result, we jump to fear, or the negative much easier and quicker than the positive. In fact, research has shown that it takes five compliments to counteract one criticism. (Parents/ grandparents, especially, keep this in mind to help your kids feel good about themselves!) This is nothing new – I know you've probably heard it before.

The human brain has also evolved, layering one part over the other. Closest to the brain stem is the reptilian brain, which controls all the automatic functions necessary for survival, such as heart rate, temperature and breathing. Layered over that is the temporal lobe, which houses the limbic system, responsible for memory and emotions. On top of that is the frontal lobe, which is the part of us that takes in information from our inner and outer world and decides what to do with it. It has also been called the executive functioning of the brain. The good news is that brain research over the last fifteen to twenty years has proven that our brains are malleable, and that our frontal lobe can continue to learn new things at any age. How does this work? Think of a well-established path that has been created in the grass from your back door to your shed in the back yard. For years you've been walking that path on the grass, and a "route" was developed where the grass stopped growing and a path was made in the dirt. Let's say you decide to move the shed to another spot in the backyard. At first there's grass on the route from your backyard to where the shed now is. In fact, you often find yourself going out the back door heading for where the shed had been for years before remembering that it's been relocated. With time, a path between the back door and where the shed now is will be created in the grass, and the old path will eventually be grown over. It's the epitome of "Use it or lose it," which explains why I can still do shorthand, which I learned in high school, because I continued taking notes with it in college, grad school and on all my jobs, but can barely recall the Spanish that I also learned in high school, even though I took Spanish for not just one year, as I had shorthand, but for all four years of high school.

The reason it's important to consider these facts at this point to reinventing yourself is to understand that to change the way your brain is wired isn't easy, but it is possible! You must change your brain wiring in order to reinvent yourself. Let's start with a fairly easy exercise that can help change the negative to the positive, or dis-empowering to empowering by changing our semantics. The semantics that we use when talking to ourselves or to others reflects our beliefs, and also affects how much stress and how much confidence we feel. The words we choose can literally make a difference whether we feel like a victim or a victor. One of the most important steps in reinventing ourselves is to move towards empowerment statements. The reason for this is that our brains do not have the capacity to make any decisions as to the validity of a statement; our brains will simply record the information as being true, and will then tell our bodies to respond as if what we say is true, thus forming a belief. A good example of this is having a dream in which you dreamt you were falling and then your foot actually kicked out and jerked you awake. Your brain didn't have the capacity to realize it was a dream so your brain told your foot what to do to "catch" yourself, although once awake, your mind was able to make the distinction.

Words to Reprogram Your Brain

Words to Reprogram (using the computer analogy) is another tool to use to start changing your thinking. There are four categories of thoughts that it would behoove you to change: Commands, Over-generalizations, Responsibility, and Catastrophizing. Changing your thinking from a word or phrase that falls under any of these categories can have amazing effects. Let's look at why this is true. Commands create a lot of stress. They are like demands over ourselves or over someone else, which imply that something needs to be different for us to feel okay. That is the reason making a preference works so well. Preferences are just that – it would be nice, but unnecessary which inherently implies that we will be okay whether the preferences are met or not. This, in and of itself, reduces the stress we experience. When thinking about the words and phrases which fall under "Commands," simply remember that it's important that we don't "should" on ourselves or others!

Over-generalizations contribute to all or nothing/black or white thinking. Words under this category can cause you to feel overwhelmed. For example, if you tell yourself that you *always* make a mistake, or that you can *never* get things right, you have just programmed your brain to continue doing what you don't want it to do. If you tell yourself that *no one* likes you, you're more than likely programming yourself to feel lonely and depressed. Sometimes these words may be used in ways that seem positive in reaching your goals, but instead create more stress, which prevents optimum functioning. For example, telling yourself that you can *never* make a mistake or that you *always* have to be perfect, puts you under a lot of negative stress or distress. Recognizing that there are no absolutes helps you to do and feel your best.

The words and phrases under Responsibility are especially important for re-inventing yourself. Playing the "Blame Game" – by putting the responsibility onto others for our feelings and reactions – is disempowering. For example, if I told my friend Joe that he gives me a headache, then I'm making Joe responsible for taking that headache away! By recognizing that I caused myself to feel or think a certain way gives me the **power** to do something about it! I would much rather have my own power and control than give it away, wouldn't you?

Catastrophizing is likewise disempowering. We become like Eeyore of Winnie the Pooh fame. Remember that our brains do not recognize our *intention* but rather our *attention.* Consequently, if we are focused on the negatives and limiting words, those are the conditions that will manifest in our lives. Conversely, programming ourselves to handle what occurs creates that reality instead, and a sense of hopefulness.

Reflect on the changes that Ilene made using the concepts noted above. When Ilene first started working with me, she consistently created great stress for herself by saying what she should have done, i.e. "I *should* have stopped him [Darryl] from having the stupid operation." She added even more distress by focusing on the notion that "Darryl *shouldn't* have died." Ilene disempowered herself by the use of over-generalizations because she said to herself she could *never* understand what Darryl had tried to teach her regarding the business, and she thought that she would *never* find friends in her community or that she had *no* life without Darryl. Catastrophizing was especially prevalent in her thinking process, as evidenced by her lamenting that "Tomorrow will be just as *horrible.*" As I worked with Ilene to change her semantics from the wording on the right side of the "Words to Reprogram" tool to those on the left, I could literally hear her calming down over the telephone.

In the Exercise below, look at the words on the right side of the page. Whenever you catch yourself using any of those words, stop or cancel them out and switch to the suggestions on the left. Since in the English language *we* read from left to right, the words we want to focus upon, or think of first, are on the left side of the page. Just like bicycle riding or driving a car, with practice, using the empowering statements becomes second nature.

WORDS TO REPROGRAM TOOL

COMMANDS

WORDS AND PHRASES TO USE	WORDS AND PHRASES TO CANCEL
I prefer…	Should (not)
I want…	Must
I would like it if…	Ought to, Have to

OVER-GENERALIZATIONS

WORDS AND PHRASES TO USE	WORDS AND PHRASES TO CANCEL
Sometimes	Always
A lot	Never
Often	No one, None
Some people	Everyone, All

RESPONSIBILITY

WORDS AND PHRASES TO USE	WORDS AND PHRASES TO CANCEL
I am responsible for…	You make me ______ (i.e., angry, sick)

I chose to feel…	It's so-and-so's fault, not mine
I made myself feel…	That makes me_____ (i.e., angry, sick)

CATASTROPHIZING

WORDS AND PHRASES TO USE	WORDS AND PHRASES TO CANCEL
I can handle it	The worst
It's OK to make mistakes	Horrible
It's OK to…	Terrible
I would prefer___, and it's OK if…	Unfair, Impossible, Can't

(Make copies of Appendix B)

"We are addicted to our thoughts. We cannot change anything if we cannot change our thinking."

~Santosh Kalwar

How Thoughts Work

To change our thinking on deep levels, it's important to realize that the brain records everything that has ever happened to us, whether we are consciously aware of it or not. There are stories of people awakening from comas who heard what was being said and what was going on around them. (Remember this fact should you ever be around someone asleep or (hopefully not) in a coma – be careful what you say because they will hear it, even if they don't consciously remember it.) Carol, the sister of a very good friend of mine, was in a coma for three months due to an aneurysm at age 20. When Carol regained consciousness, she could remember that her parents and family were present and that they never gave up hope that she would regain consciousness. Now in her sixties, although she has limitations due to her brain trauma, Carol is one of the happiest people I have ever met. She is a good example to keep in mind when we further our discussion on how thoughts influence feelings later on in this book. There was another woman I used to know named Sallie, who had an operation to remove her gall bladder (back in the day when gall bladder surgery involved making a rather large incision and not just a little pinhole). Previous to the operation, Sallie had liked her doctor and trusted him. Afterwards, although the operation was successful, Sallie had an intense dislike for the doctor and didn't want to see him for her follow-up appointments. Sallie had no explanation for this change of attitude, and it bothered her so much that she actually enlisted the help of a hypnotherapist. Through that process, Sallie recalled the doctor saying in the operating room, "If she [Sallie] weren't so damn fat, we'd be over this operation a lot quicker!" Becomes pretty understandable why Sallie didn't like her doctor anymore, huh?

So, our brain records through our five physical senses everything that we have experienced, whether we are consciously aware of it or not. But here's the thing – the brain is really a slave to the mind. While the brain does the recording and tells the body how to behave accordingly, it is the mind that interprets the meaning of one's experiences and tells or programs the brain what to do about those experiences. While science has proven that we can rewire our brains, it's our minds that we need to convince, which in a previous chapter you learned was the programmer of the brain. The thing is, our minds like to be right! Our minds will do almost anything to prove that we are right, whether or not circumstances have changed. It's the reason it's so difficult to give up our truth (Telling and Re-telling our Understanding of what we Think Happened); we have told and re-told our understanding of what happened so often that we have convinced ourselves that that is the only way to see something. The way to change our minds is simple – to change our minds we must change our thoughts. But don't confuse simple with easy. Our typical way of thinking, our old paradigms, will keep holding us back if we let them. That's because they have created a wide and deep path in our brains from constant use. It takes diligence to let the "grass" grow over the old path and to keep "walking" down the newly created path. Our Why to seeing something differently and thus behaving differently has to be very strong in order for our minds to even be willing to give it a try.

Up until now, you may have thought things worked kind of like this: Something happens, someone says something or does something, and that "something" makes you feel a certain way. Your body will react. If you felt hurt, you may cry. Another response to being hurt is to get angry. (An aside here – anger is a secondary emotion – it only occurs because we are either hurt or frustrated; frustration being the result of not being able to reach a goal.) The anger may manifest itself as a feeling in your body that you are about to explode – and you may, indeed, explode either verbally or physically. If you are embarrassed, your face may turn red. Here's an illustration of this phenomenon:

Event → Feelings →Body/Behavior

But actually, there is something else that occurs between the Event and the Feelings: It's a Thought. So the more accurate illustration is:

Event →Thought→Feelings→Body/Behavior

Here's an easily understandable example: Let's say the Event is that it is snowing outside. How would you feel about that? If you enjoy winter sports, or it's Christmas Eve, or snow in your area would cause you to get a day off of work, you might be feeling happy about the Event. I personally never liked winter, the cold or the snow, which also factored into my desire to move to North Carolina. So while you may be happy that it is snowing, I would be unhappy. The Event is the same but our feelings are the polar (pun again intended) opposite because what we *think* about the fact or event of snow is different.

How strong our thoughts are about an event affects the strength of our emotions. The stronger the thought, the stronger the emotion. Thoughts gather energy. The energy becomes stronger just by thinking more about a particular thought. Ever have an argument with someone and the more you think about it, the more upset you become? Conversely, the more you think about a happy thought, such as when first falling in love, the more you think or focus on how wonderful that person is, the happier you become. That's because the same part of the brain that holds memory, the limbic system, is the same part of the brain that holds emotion. That's the reason that having a memory of an event will trigger the same emotional reaction as you originally had. I call this phenomenon The Thought Cycle. It goes like this:

thought →energy→reality→thought→energy→reality, etc.

Changing Your Thoughts

The more we dwell on the thought, the stronger the thought becomes. Now when it's a pleasant or empowering thought, we want to keep dwelling on it. When it's an unpleasant one, if we keep dwelling on it, it can negatively affect how we experience the rest of our day or longer. So here's the trick. When you have a thought you don't want to dwell upon, STOP it between its first occurrence and its ongoing occurrences; that is, before it gathers Energy. You can do this by telling yourself to STOP, to DELETE, or to CANCEL that thought. However, we cannot not think! That is, after stopping or cancelling the first thought, unless you replace the original thought with another more empowering thought, the original thought will keep coming back. By creating another more empowering thought, you eliminate the original disempowering or negative thought since it's absolutely impossible to simultaneously have two opposing thoughts. Opposing thoughts might occur one after another in less than a nano-second, but they cannot exist at the very same time. For example, every time Ilene told me that she felt depressed and anxious, she also had been dwelling on feeling powerless without Darryl. I would then remind her of what she had already accomplished, such as being able to drive to her sister's, or of the friends she had since made, and as the focus of her thoughts changed, her mood lightened and she would feel better.

Let's practice this with an easy illustration. Right now I want you to think about anything BUT a pink elephant with purple spots. What did you see? Of course, a pink elephant with purple spots. Our brains can't comprehend a negative command. Now, every time you think of that pink elephant with purple spots, I want you to tell yourself to STOP that thought, and think instead of a blue and green giraffe. Can you do it? Of course you can - because no one but YOU can determine what you think. Initially, you may find that you are thinking about the elephant before remembering that you want to think about the giraffe instead. Kind of like that commercial, "I could have had a V-8!" The more you practice this, however, the shorter and shorter the time between thinking of the elephant and then thinking of the giraffe will become. Keep on practicing, and you'll switch to the giraffe almost immediately. It's like anything – the more we practice, the more it becomes second nature, such as learning to walk, riding a bicycle, or driving a car. Initially we have to think about what we are doing, then we over-compensate for a while, like turning the steering wheel or handle bars too much in the opposite direction until we learn how to keep the car down the middle of the lane or the bike upright. After a while, we have muscle memory and we no longer have to consciously think about how to keep our balance on a bike or negotiate a sharp turn in a car. It comes naturally. So will changing your thoughts, if you just keep practicing.

Now let's see how this applies to actual happenings in your life. Let's say after two years of being divorced from your husband of twenty years, you decide you are ready to try dating again. You had been reluctant to date, but friends had been wanting to fix you up and promised that the person they had in mind was a really nice guy. You muster up all your courage, agree to meet him, and although inwardly you had been shaking in your boots, you had a really good time. Mr. Nice Guy said he had a good time, too, and he said he would call you the next day to see about going out on his boat. You're feeling pretty excited and perhaps just like a teenager again. It's a great feeling especially after the train wreck of your marriage. Then Mr. Nice Guy doesn't call you back like he had said he would. Your happiness bubble pops! You might even feel sad, hurt, or angry when you didn't hear from him. You might have even told friends about it so you could get support for how rotten it was that he didn't call you or so you can be justified in your feelings. Maybe you told the friends who had originally fixed you up with him so that they would know that he really was Mr. No-Goodnik. Right now you're probably thinking to yourself that, of course, anyone, especially in the same circumstance, would feel the same way. But wait! Let's say that the friends who had introduced you found out that their friend, Mr. Nice Guy, had received a call that morning from the nursing home where his father lived and that it was critical that he get to the nursing home right away. Would that change your feelings? Why? The event was still the same. Oh, because now that you knew what happened, you can understand that Mr. Nice Guy, being such a nice guy, ran off to see his possibly dying father. What changed? Not your brain, certainly. Oh, you changed your mind about what it meant that he hadn't called you. In other words, you changed your thoughts! You are now saying to yourself that it's perfectly understandable, and that his not calling *had nothing to do with you*! Guess what? Not only have you changed your mind because you changed your thoughts, but you had the power all along to change your thoughts! We humans are given what the rest of the animal kingdom isn't...the right to choose what we think. How awesome is that? We have the power within us to change our thoughts at any time! You could have told yourself all along that his not calling you back had nothing to do with you, that it was his loss, that he was probably busy, or any myriad of things which would have enabled you to feel better. Do you realize how powerful this ability is? It means that the ability to reinvent yourself lies within you! No one else can make you think anything – it's all up to you!

"Pay attention to your thinking, and change it in areas that you don't have peace. By doing so, you'll bring more happiness into your life and to those around you."

~Louise Hay and David Kessler,
You Can Heal Your Heart

SELF-TALK TOOL:

Describe an Event factually. (Remember Dragnet? "Just the facts, ma'am.") This means to describe what occurred without any judgment or interpretation. For example, instead of the event being, "My sister acted like a jerk," you would write down, "My sister said that she didn't like my new outfit." In other words, describe it as anyone who overheard this exchange would describe it.

Your turn; describe an incident that recently occurred which was unpleasant to experience:

Event, stated factually:

____

____

____

Now get in touch with your thoughts by recalling what you were saying to yourself. For example, you may have being saying /thinking, "My sister is always criticizing me. She has our whole life. She always acts like a 'know-it-all. She is such a jerk!" Now your turn:

What did I say/think to myself when this event occurred:

____

____

____

Next is to get in touch with how you felt as a result of what you were thinking/saying to yourself: "How did I feel, what emotion was I experiencing, as a result of what I was thinking?" (A note of caution here: write down just an emotion, [see appendix C for an extensive list of possible emotions].) In American vernacular, we often use "I feel" to describe a thought instead of an emotion. If you can substitute the word "think" for the word "feel" you are not describing an emotion; another clue that you are describing a thought instead of a feeling or emotion is if you can insert the words "that," "as if," or "like" after the words "I feel."

I feel/felt (emotion only):

____

____

____

Next, what was the reason behind what you were thinking/saying to yourself? Now we get back into our thoughts. However, this is probably a bunch of thoughts put together which have created "Our story" or a Belief that we have from which we have been operating. (Remember truth is Telling and Retelling our Understanding of what we Think Happened.)

Continuing with the example of your sister, the story that you have been telling yourself is that "My sister has always told me what to do. Being the big sister she thinks she knows best. She has always been controlling."

I felt that way because:

____

____

____

The complete exercise goes together like this:

Event, stated factually:

____

____

____

What did I say/think to myself when this event occurred:

____

____

____

I feel/felt (emotion only):

____

____

____

Because:

____

____

____

(Make copies of Appendix C)

Now using the same template, and the same event, reframe what you say/think to yourself. You can utilize Words to Reprogram to help with this. Notice how you are now feeling after writing out the new reframe. You are probably feeling a higher level emotion than you had before, right? If not, keep writing down reframes until your feelings have shifted to a higher vibration. (If you're not sure what I mean by a higher vibration, tune into your body and note if you are feeling a sense of expansion or one of contraction. Higher vibrations always produce a sense of expansiveness, a lightness, a joy. More on that in a subsequent chapter.) While the event that occurred remains the same, it is your feelings that have changed because your thoughts have changed, just as in the Dating Mr. Good Guy example.

Using Positive Affirmations

I wouldn't be surprised if you have already heard of using Positive Affirmations, which are also useful in creating reframes to help ourselves feel better. These are positive or empowering thoughts, or your blue and green giraffes, if you will. Below is a list of affirmations that you may find useful in reprogramming your brain. Circle no more than three of them that really resonate with you. You can take one from each category, or all three from one area; whatever you choose, but for right now, only use three. Whatever resonates with you is personally *for* you; it is your intuition or Higher Self letting you know what you need, just as your doctor taking your blood or doing a hair analysis can indicate what minerals or vitamins would be best for you to take.

POSITIVE AFFIRMATIONS TOOL:

POSITIVE AFFIRMATIONS ON ACCEPTANCE

- Each day I do the best that I can; it is enough to have done my best
- I accept who I am
- Even though I have had negative experiences in the past, I am still a good person
- I've already been through other painful experiences, and I survived

- This, too, shall pass
- Although my feelings make me uncomfortable right now, I can accept them
- I can be anxious and still deal with the situation
- This is an opportunity for me to learn how to cope with my feelings/fears
- My anxiety/fear/sadness/anger won't kill me; it just doesn't feel good right now
- It's okay to feel sad/anxious/afraid/angry sometimes
- I deserve to be happy
- I deserve to be loved

POSITIVE AFFIRMATIONS ON CHOICE AND CHANGE

- I have the power to change myself
- I can make my own choices and decisions
- I am free to choose to live as I wish and to give priority to my desires
- I can choose happiness whenever I wish, no matter what my circumstances
- I am flexible and open to change in every aspect of my life
- My thoughts don't control my life; I do
- I can think different thoughts if I want to
- I'm not in danger right now
- I'm strong and I can deal with this
- I care about myself and other people
- I act with confidence
- I love myself

POSITIVE AFFIRMATIONS ON MY PURPOSE

- I'm here for a reason
- There's a purpose to my life, even though I might not always see it

*Various affirmations taken from The Dialectical Behavior Therapy Skills Workbook by Marsha Linehan, and from The Relaxation and Stress Management Workbook by McKay, Davis & Fanning

HOW TO USE THE AFFIRMATIONS TOOL

Here are my recommendations on how to use the three affirmations you have chosen:

- Hand print, don't use cursive or your computer, to write out each affirmation on either an index card or a Post-It note. (Hand printing helps to imprint our brains faster and easier.)
- Put all three affirmations on one card or note or choose to print each out on a separate card or note.
- Put the affirmations by your bedside, either on or in your nightstand.
- Also make a copy to carry with you, in a notebook, wallet, or pocketbook. If you live in an environment which allows you to comfortably do this, post them also by your bathroom mirror and/or any other location that you see daily, such as the dash of your car.
- First thing upon awakening and right before going to sleep, read the affirmations that are by your bedside. As you read them, imagine feeling as if they are already true. Feel it, see it, and believe it, just as you are to do with your vision. The imagining and the feeling as if it's true are critical to this

process. Getting resistance from your ego, like a little voice saying "That's not true" is perfectly normal at first. However, the more you imprint or program the new affirmations, the more your brain and mind will accept them. You are creating a new life path in your mind, brain, and body.

How Jennifer Used This Tool to Reinvent Herself: Jennifer was feeling anxious. "What else is new?" Jennifer asked herself. She felt she had been anxious her entire life, and she was sick and tired of it, but she didn't know what to do about it. Jennifer decided to work with me so she could stop her chronic anxiety. Part of her didn't believe it was possible, but another part of her knew she had to do something! She had never heard of the idea that she could change her feelings if she changed her thoughts and what she was picturing in her mind, but the concepts really resonated with her. In a relatively short period of time, Jennifer was able to catch her thoughts that created anxiety, and using the Thought Cycle, stop them from gathering energy. "Is there any evidence that this thought is true?" Jennifer would ask herself. Realizing that there wasn't any, Jennifer diligently practiced the replacement thoughts of: "I can think different thoughts if I want to; I'm really not in danger right now," and "I can remain calm and peaceful." Along with some deep breathing exercises that I taught her, Jennifer was able to stop the anxiety that she had experienced her entire life. She felt like a new person!

Points to Ponder:

"We are shaped by our thoughts, we become what we think.

When the mind is pure, joy follows like a shadow that never leaves."

~Buddha

"Our thoughts are our creative power. Whatever we persistently focus our thoughts and feelings upon, manifests in our lives."

~Unity Principle #3

If you would like additional assistance in learning how to use these tools, please contact me by email:

Trudy@TruestLifeCoaching.com or calling 336-763-4611.

CHAPTER 7:
STEP TWO: CHANGING BELIEFS

"A belief is not merely an idea that the mind possesses. It is an idea that possesses the mind."

~**Robert Oxton Bolton**

"Your beliefs rule your thoughts and thoughts shape reality – choose your beliefs carefully."

~**Abraham-Hicks,**
Law of Attraction, Pearl of Wisdom #9

While I previously equated Belief with Faith about something not yet seen, in this chapter beliefs (plural) mean a conglomeration or coalescence of thoughts that you believe to be true. It's important to realize that *beliefs* do not equal *facts*. Ilene thinking she couldn't have a meaningful life without Darryl wasn't true; likewise, Jennifer constantly thinking she was in danger was not true. Christopher Columbus would not have been able to journey across the ocean if the prevalent belief of his era had been fact; if he had believed it, he would never have sailed across the ocean blue in 1492. Remember Roger Bannister and the subsequent runners who ran a mile in under four minutes because their beliefs in the possibility had changed? More recently, I watched the 25th season of "Dancing with the Stars." Former Paralympic champion, Victoria Arlen, who just 18 months before dancing on the show had been in a wheelchair, danced so well that she made it to the semi-finals. Although not able to feel her legs, she danced absolutely beautifully. (Personally, I thought she deserved to be in the finals…just sayin') In telling her story on the show, Victoria stated that when she was in an almost completely vegetative state she told herself that there was going to be more to her story. She is an epitome of how positive thoughts create positive beliefs which affect the body and behavior. She truly has reinvented herself!

Unless you discern how your collection of thoughts have coalesced into limiting beliefs, you will not be able to refute the beliefs that no longer serve you. In her previous life, Ilene had believed that she could not drive to visit her sister or fly to visit friends without Darryl with her. Ilene's belief held her back from a more fulfilling life even when Darryl was alive. It was only after his death that Ilene allowed herself to let go of the limiting belief and replace it with a more empowering one in order to reinvent her life. The pain of staying in her comfort zone now outweighed her growing pains! She felt the fear, and did something new anyway. I have a friend and colleague, Sharon, who decided in her sixties to give up the vintage retail shop that she owned in order to reinvent herself as a mental health therapist. She went to undergrad and then graduate school to become the excellent mental health therapist that she now is. Another client, Florence, 55, is now fully engaged in her passion of flipping houses. It took a messy and at-the-time unwanted break up with her business partner for Florence to believe she could run the business on her own.

Beliefs are always in the background running us. If they are empowering beliefs, celebrate! Often, however, we carry limiting beliefs about which we are unaware. Whatever beliefs we have affect how we see the world and our place in it. We interpret what is occurring in the present by what has happened to us in the past and how we felt about it. Our brains scan the environment for what is similar, and our minds interpret what is in the environment according to what happened before; in other words, by what we believe. We notice what we are searching for, and don't even notice what does not fit into our picture of the truth. For example, have you ever bought a new car and then noticed that make everywhere? That happened to me when I bought a Honda Fit. After I told the Honda dealer about my requirements for a car, which had to fit a lot of equipment for the job I had at the time as well as have low gas mileage, the dealer introduced me to the Fit, which I had never heard of before. After I bought it, I saw Honda Fits all over the place, but had never noticed them before.

In addition, we will recall information by what we have interpreted to be important. Have you ever reminisced with a sibling or a good friend about an event, and you had totally different recollections of what occurred, or maybe one of you recalled it vividly and the other one didn't? Of course you have. I have four good friends from grammar school who live across the United States, and with whom I get together for a reunion every other year. None of these friends remember how they dumped me during seventh and eighth grade, and then became friends with me again in high school. Being dumped by this group of friends in junior high was very traumatic for me, and probably had a lot to do with my lack of self-worth during my pre-teens, and even my decision to become a licensed clinical social worker (for ten years I worked in school systems, I think to help kids who were suffering as I had been.) But not one of these very intelligent, caring women remembers not being friends with me during seventh and eighth grade!

Our beliefs affect whether we see ourselves as a victim or a victor. I like to use the following acronyms to delineate the two terms: Victim means the Vision I c, troubles in me. Victor means the Vision I c, transformation of reality. Whether we believe ourselves to be a victim or a victor forms the story on which we base our lives. The story may start from an actual occurrence which we attach meaning to afterwards, thus creating a belief, and then we keep adding meaning not only to the original event but also to subsequent occurrences that support the original erroneous belief. For example, for a long time I saw myself as a victim in my marriage to Ray. When I started owning my power in the relationship, I became a victor – which was a transformation of my reality. Yes, in my case it meant ending the marriage in order to fully enjoy that transformation, but I still feel it was worth it.

How Annalise Reinvented Herself by Changing Her Beliefs: I worked with a woman, Annalise, who was in her mid-thirties at the time, who had been raped in her early twenties. Annalise added the following beliefs to being raped: I am unworthy, I am stupid, I am not a good person, and she also believed that her husband likewise had to be a "bad" person for staying with her when she was so damaged. Her story was not only affecting her sense of self-worth but also her marriage. In working with Annalise she was eventually able to let go of all the additional stories she had added to the first event. Although being raped is traumatic, Annalise was able to say "I was raped" without it meaning anything else.

One powerful way to eradicate a core belief is to tell your complete story with all the subsequent beliefs you have added to it, to someone who is understanding. While you could tell the story to someone whom you trust implicitly who will hold sacred space and keep what you say confidential, I encourage you do this exercise with a therapist. Initially, as you tell the story with all the subsequent meanings you have attached to it, there may be a lot of emotion rising. As discussed earlier, the limbic system of the brain that stores memory also stores emotion, so whatever you felt at the time of the original occurrence will keep coming up. Continue to tell the story out loud, nonetheless. As you continue to tell the story, the emotion gets drained from it. You will actually get bored with it and it will lose its negative power over you. You might also want to do The Work by Byron Katie, and ask yourself if there is any evidence that what you have attached to the original occurrence is true. As you begin to realize there is no evidence that your beliefs have any validity, eventually the story collapses to just the original event. So what did it mean that Annalise was raped – just that: Annalise was raped. It had nothing to do with her worthiness, her intelligence or her womanhood. Although it was still an unfortunate incident, Annalise was able to let go of her beliefs about the event. When she let the beliefs go, not only did her sense of self-worth improve, but so did her marriage. In fact, after letting go of these beliefs, Annalise left her low-paying job in a non-profit agency to go to law school. Last I heard, Annalise was a very happy lawyer with a good marriage.

Another powerful technique to reduce suffering caused by the meanings we have attached to our stories is taken from the work of Colin Tipping, the creator of Radical Forgiveness®. According to Tipping, the story about what the original event means is all B.S. (Belief System). Our suffering comes from our beliefs and we have a choice as to whether or not we want to continue to suffer. In sum, change the story, so you change the beliefs in order to reduce or eliminate the suffering. Tipping has developed excellent worksheets which take you through this process. For more on how to apply this technique, I strongly recommend the book Radical Forgiveness, by Colin Tipping, or go to www.radicalforgiveness.com. There are a lot of freebies you can download that will help. There are also listings of Radical Forgiveness Coaches and Radical Forgiveness Practitioners, of which I am one. If you think you would like support in this process, I encourage you to contact me or to seek someone else trained in Radical Forgiveness to do this work with you.

It is critical to bring your limiting beliefs to conscious awareness in order to change them. Several well-known therapists, such as Albert Ellis, David Burns, and Aaron Beck have determined that there are some basic limiting beliefs that people may hold. (For more information, look up Rational Emotive Therapy or Cognitive Behavior Therapy.)

LIMITING BELIEFS TOOL

In the following exercise, please read through the beliefs and circle the number of the ones that resonate with you. The belief has been abbreviated into a short statement. (In the parentheses I have elaborated a little on a belief which I thought might have needed further clarification.)

Note: In all the years of doing this exercise with clients, I haven't found anyone who does not hold at least one of these beliefs; likewise, I haven't found anyone who holds all of them.

1. Everyone must love me. (It is an absolute necessity that I have love and approval from peers, family, and friends: I am wrong or bad if they don't love or approve of me.)
2. I must be good at everything. (I must be unfailingly competent and almost perfect in all that I undertake.) Note: Perfectionists will resonate with this one.

3. When people don't do what they should, they should get what's coming to them. (Certain people are evil, wicked and villainous, and should be punished.)
4. Things should be different. (It is horrible when people and things are not the way I want them to be; there is only one good or right way to do something – my way!)
5. It's your fault I feel this way. (Naturally, external events cause me to react the way I do.)
6. I know something bad will happen. (I feel fear or anxiety about anything that is unknown, uncertain, or potentially dangerous.)
7. It's easier not to try. (It is easier to avoid life's problems than to face life's difficulties and responsibilities.) If you have circled this belief, please add your standard excuses to avoid responsibility here:

   ____

   ____

   ____

8. I need someone stronger than I am. (I can't make independent judgments or express my needs without relying on someone smarter/in authority, etc.)
9. I can't help being this way; I can't change. (Because of what happened in my past, it is natural for me to be the way I am and there's nothing I can do about it.)
10. I am such a good person that your problem is my problem. (I take responsibility for other people's problems, especially people I care about. I would be selfish otherwise.) Note: Moms, in particular, may get sucked into this one.
11. I am helpless and have no control over what I feel. (i.e., Of course, I am depressed and anxious; I can't help it.)

12. I must get along with everyone because I couldn't stand it if I hurt someone. (Self-sacrifice is necessary because my needs and wants are not as important as keeping the peace.)
13. I know that good relationships are based on mutual sacrifice and focus on giving. (I must constantly deny myself because it is better to give than to receive.)
14. I can't express my real self or my needs. (I have to please others no matter what the cost so that I will not be abandoned or rejected.)
15. Being alone is horrible. (I cannot be happy, have pleasure or be fulfilled when/if I am alone.)
16. I cannot be happy unless I have the perfect relationship with someone who loves me.
17. Life is not fair because X happened to me. I should never feel pain; I am entitled to a good life.
18. My worth depends on how much I have achieved and produced.
19. I should never feel anger because it is automatically bad and destructive.
20. If I am selfish in any way, I am bad or wrong.
21. I don't have to express myself or communicate because that person (my spouse, partner, child, good friend, etc.) should know what I am thinking. (I know what they think because I know them so well and they should know what I am thinking, too.)
22. Everyone else is doing so much better than I am. (I see only the good and positive aspects in others and when I compare myself to them, I don't measure up.) Note: Social media helps perpetuate this belief because we start to compare our insides with everyone else's outsides.

23. Because X happened, I must be a bad, worthless, or undeserving person. (I must be a bad person because something painful happened to me.) Note: Annalise was stuck here.

(Make copies of Appendix E)

Beliefs are just habits of how we think, and no matter how long we have held those beliefs and habits, with persistency and consistency, they can be changed. First we need the Desire to change them, then the Belief (faith) that we can change them, and then the Expectancy (vision) of the change. If you don't have the desire to actually change the belief, you can take it back a step to "Want to Want to." For example, a smoker probably knows that she *should* stop smoking because it is healthier to do so. (By the way, it's important to not "should" on yourself!) However, the smoker may really enjoy the habit especially in a social setting, or the smoker may be concerned that she will gain weight if she quits smoking, or simply can't believe that she could ever be a non-smoker. Her Desire consequently is compromised. To build up her Desire to stop smoking, she can affirm that her Desire to quit smoking is growing daily, thereby flaming the Desire to quit instead of flaming the cigarette!

HOW TO USE WORDS TO REPROGRAM BELIEFS TOOL

- Using the Words to Reprogram Exercise from the previous chapter, change any and all of the Words to Cancel (on the right side of the page) inherent within the Belief statements you circled to the Words to Use (on the left side of the page) in each of the beliefs you have circled.
- Then write a statement refuting the limiting belief that needs to be changed. For example, take Belief #1, "Everyone must

love me." What words need to be changed? "Everyone" because it is an Over-generalization, and "must" because it is a Command. The belief could be changed to "I like it when I get love/appreciation/approval from other people." Or "I know that I am okay whether or not someone approves of me." Or "I am happy that some people approve of me." There are any number of words and phrases you can use.

- Be sure to:
  1. State what you want instead of what you don't want,
  2. Use only words or statements from the left-hand column of the Words to Reprogram sheet instead of the right-hand side
  3. Create statements using the present tense. If you use a future tense, you are putting your positive feelings off to the future rather than experiencing them now.
  4. Hand print your new belief out on an index card or Post-It note, and utilize the cards or Post-Its the same way that I suggested for the Positive Affirmations Exercise.
  5. As you read the new beliefs, imagine that you already believe the new belief; feel the feelings as if the belief is already true. Again, initially there might be some resistance because, by definition, beliefs are habitual ways of thinking – and habits like to hold on. However, keep reading, feeling and imagining the new belief/way of being until you have accepted it as true.

This process can take about 30 days so keep on keeping on. You will love your new reinvented way of being and your new truEST life. I promise!

CHAPTER 8: STEPS THREE AND FOUR: CHANGING FEELINGS AND VIBES

"All that is required is that you pay attention to the way you feel, and that you let yourself be drawn to those things that feel good or right to you while you let yourself be moved away from those things that do not."

~Abraham-Hicks

"Happiness is not something you chase and catch. It's something you choose."

~Steven Aitchison

In the previous chapters, I mentioned that it's important to change your feelings based on your new thoughts, paradigms and beliefs. I really want to emphasize the importance of doing so – changing your feelings is where the magic happens.

So let's go back to satisfying the Left brain hemisphere as to why this is so. Within and surrounding our bodies is an electro-magnetic field. If we change our inner feelings, our electro-magnetic field changes. There is a shift in energy, and that energy pulls into our experiences whatever matches that energy. Think of a tuning fork; as you twang one tuning fork it has a tone caused by its vibration; any tuning fork in the vicinity will begin to vibrate at the same frequency. So think of feelings as your tuning fork. Ask yourself what you want to bring into your life, and then tune into the feelings to create the vibrations that match what you want. An important note here: Think of what you want instead of what you don't want. Often we focus on the "Don't want" but our brains, as well as the Universe, have difficulty comprehending a negative command. Think of a small child – if you tell the child "Don't run in the house!" what happens? The child is more than likely to keep on running until you are exasperated. The child isn't trying to be deliberately disobedient. Instead, realize that it just takes a while for his or her brain to comprehend what was said. Our brains think in pictures, so when you say "Don't run!" to the child, his or her brain actually pictures running. Instead, tell the child what you want, such as "Please just walk when you're inside the house. It's fine to run in the backyard." See what results you will get. This is true for our brains and for the Universe as well. So when you say either out loud or to yourself, "I don't want...whatever" our brains picture the "whatever," and Spirit/the Universe/God will pick up on the energy of what you don't want instead of what you do want. Remember that the Universe gives us what we have placed our *attention* upon, regardless of our *intention.*

A key principle to reinventing yourself or to changing an unwanted condition is to realize that you don't have to change the condition, you just have to stop focusing on or thinking about it. If you keep attending to what you don't want, in addition to magnetizing what you don't want, your feelings will stay at a lower-level, which means that the created vibration will continue to be low. Please remember that even the slightest shift of focus to anything unpleasant not only pulls in the undesired consequences of that negative focus, but also creates a barrier between you and receiving the good that is already there. Recognize that the only purpose of unwanted conditions is to warn you about how you are flowing your energy. Employing the Thought Cycle can be of help here. Rather than continuing to energize the thought of the unwanted condition, find something else, *anything* else, to think about that will get you to feeling even a tiny bit better than you do at the present, and make that switch. It could be a thought unrelated to the situation as long as the emotion that the thought engenders is positive. So you can think about an upcoming vacation, or the cuteness of your grandchildren, or the antics of your silly dog or precocious cat. Stay with that new thought-picture until you feel your mood change. You can also pick a high frequency, pleasant feeling such as gratitude or appreciation to focus upon.

Once you feel your mood switch to the positive, talk out loud about what condition you do want instead. In other words, change your feeling state *first* before enfolding your reinvented self and the life that you want into what you are picturing. As you imagine being your reinvented self, and following your truEST life path, what do you look like? What are you wearing? Where are you? What are you doing? Who is in your life? Take a moment now to play with this. You may want to incorporate what you wrote in your Vision; refer back to Chapter 4 and see and feel how what you wrote now fits. You may want to change it, tweak it, or find that it's still exactly what you want. You can also use the Self-Talk exercise that you learned in Chapter 6 on Changing Thoughts to help you with this. Regardless of how you get the picture, imagine yourself as you want to be when your vibes are high so that you can follow your truEST life path. You don't have to know the "how-to's." Leave that up to the Universe. Just create and magnify the high-frequency emotional state. With practice you will be able to switch from the negative to the positive at the drop of a hat. As many New Thought and spiritual teachers have stated, it's not what you do, it's how you flow your energy that's important and which brings into matter what you desire. Remember: energy comes from emotions. Change your emotions and you change your energy.

Change your energy and you change your conditions to what you want.

Changing your physicality can also change your vibrations. When we are feeling down, our bodies may slump, our shoulders may round, and our faces usually are drawn tight. There are physical things that you can do to help raise your vibrational energy. One physical way to raise your vibrational energy is to smile. Not a phony smile, but a genuine tender smile, such as thinking of something that you cherish, such as holding your newborn child or grandchild, watching a puppy play, or watching a feel-good movie. Another is to stand tall, fist pump or high five in the air, or to jump up and down excitedly, like your favorite team just won (Go, Cubbies!) One of my favorite ways for kick-starting positive vibrations is to listen to music that I love and that makes me feel happy. For most people, their happy music is the music that was popular when they were teenagers (providing the lyrics are still upbeat; so if rap was popular when you were a teen, be sure that the music you select has positive messages.) For myself, I play music from the sixties when I'm cleaning my house. Since I'm not what you would call Susie Homemaker, playing my sixties music keeps my vibes upbeat while doing something that is generally not my favorite activity. For more exploration on ways to flow energy positively, I suggest you read the works of Lynn Grabhorn.

Another great resource is the works of Esther and Jerry Hicks, who received information from Abraham, a group of loving non-physical entities, which, along with the movie and book, The Secret, popularized the Law of Attraction. In their book, Ask and It Is Given, Abraham taught how to use your Emotional Guidance System. As explained by Abraham, "...the emotional guidance scale is a scale of our feelings and emotions, in sequence from our highest vibrational feelings to our lowest. According to Abraham, if we feel our emotions are on the lower end of the scale, it is necessary to move our emotions up the scale in order to create higher vibrations with which to create our lives. Abraham recommends that we move slowly up the scale rather than jumping straight to #1, as it would be too much of a disconnect, and consequently too difficult to do. For example, when I was a school social worker, I would work with students who were failing about ways to think of themselves as "C" students. It would have been too difficult to go from seeing themselves as "F" students to "A" students. However, once they had made the necessary thought, belief and action changes to actually become "C" students, I could then work with them on becoming "A" students. Likewise, if there is too much of a gap between where you are now with your feelings and your current conditions, you may want to move up the emotional scale slightly and also envision improvement with current conditions rather than picturing the perfect conditions you seek. This helps your logical left brain hemisphere accept new thoughts, paradigms and visions without too much push-back. The push-back is what can prevent you from being able to manifest what you want. It's like planting a new seed in the ground; with the right amount of sun and water you would expect it to grow. However, if you kept digging up the seed to check on its progress, you would actually be inhibiting its ability to grow. Personally, I think our Belief (Faith) comes into play here. If we have enough Belief, we could go straight to the top, as the great Way Shower, Jesus, was able to do. However, for most of us, we need to take smaller steps to fit within the faith that we have. So rather than having lack of faith, increase your Belief a step at a time.

Below is the Abraham Emotional Guidance Scale as given to Esther and Jerry Hicks and presented in their book, Ask and It Is Given. Using Abraham's scale below, identify where you might be on the Emotional Guidance Scale at this moment:

EMOTIONAL SCALE:

1. Joy/Appreciation/Empowered/Freedom/Love
2. Passion
3. Enthusiasm/Eagerness/Happiness
4. Positive Expectation/Belief
5. Optimism
6. Hopefulness
7. Contentment
8. Boredom
9. Pessimism
10. Frustration/Irritation/Impatience
11. Overwhelment
12. Disappointment
13. Doubt
14. Worry
15. Blame
16. Discouragement
17. Anger
18. Revenge
19. Hatred/Rage
20. Jealousy
21. Insecurity/Guilt/Unworthiness
22. Fear/Grief/Depression/Despair/Powerlessness

As previously stated, Abraham recommends climbing up the emotional scale one to two steps at a time. However, I have found it useful in working with clients to utilize the four basic emotions or categories of emotions: Mad, sad, glad, and afraid. I work with clients to bring their feelings up one level at a time within the same category of emotion in order to diffuse the emotion associated with a particular event. Below is Abraham's Emotional Guidance Scale with the slight changes I have made to it:

EMOTIONAL SCALE FOR YOUR TRUEST LIFE TOOL:

Glad

1. Joy/Appreciation/Empowered/Freedom/Love
2. Passion
3. Enthusiasm/Eagerness/Happiness
4. Positive Expectation/Belief
5. Optimism
6. Hopefulness
7. Contentment

Sad

8. Boredom
9. Pessimism
12. Disappointment
16. Discouragement
21. Guilt/Unworthiness
22. Grief/Depression/Despair/Powerlessness

Mad

10. Frustration/Irritation/Impatience
11. Overwhelmed

15. Blame
17. Anger
18. Revenge
19. Hatred/Rage
20. Jealousy

Afraid

13. Doubt
14. Worry
21. Insecurity
22. Fear

As you have already learned, when you find yourself at the lower end of the emotional scale you can make yourself feel better by changing your thoughts. Practice this by using the Self-Talk exercise previously suggested in this book to move yourself up the scale. Rather than trying to "just get over it and be happy," the process is to name your emotions, own them, accept them, and then let them go by replacing them with a higher-frequency emotion one step at a time until you feel better. For example, if you identify that you are feeling Fear, (22) on the scale, by using the Self-Talk exercise you could bring yourself up to Insecurity (21) which is related to Fear. You would then stay there for a while until you really feel the shift from Fear to Insecurity; and then you would be ready to bring yourself up to Worry (14). From Worry you could make the leap to Hopefulness (6), from there to Positive Expectation (4) and from there to Empowerment (1).

As you read the example below which uses the Emotional Guidance Scale combined with the Self-Talk Exercise you learned in Chapter 4 for Ilene, whom you met earlier, which helped her in the process of reinventing herself after her husband passed away, read the statements out loud. Speaking the words out loud puts more feeling into them. As you do so, notice how you are feeling.

Ilene's Example:
Event, stated factually: My husband died.

What did I say/think to myself when this event occurred? How could this happen to me? I miss him so much. He was my whole life. I've never been alone before. I don't know what to do. I don't know how to take care of myself without him; the future is scary; I can't do this.

I felt (emotion only): Fear/Grief/Depression/Despair/Powerlessness (22)

(Notice that Ilene's feelings, while understandable, are all emotions that are on the bottom of the scale.) To make this exercise easier to use as an example, for now I'll just utilize Ilene's feelings of Fear and Powerlessness rather than Grief and Depression.

What can I think and say to myself, instead, to help me feel better? Even if I'm not sure how to handle things right now, that doesn't mean I can't learn how.

I feel (emotion only): Insecurity (21)

Next, what can I now think and say to myself to help me feel better yet? I'm learning new things and growing every day.

I feel (emotion only): Worry (14)

Before moving up the Emotional Scale again, this might be a good time for Ilene to use the envisioning process since our brains think in pictures. Worry is imagining that something "bad" or unpleasant is going to happen in the future. So in the scenario above, it would be helpful for Ilene to envision what she wants to experience in her future instead of picturing the future negatively. Ilene could choose to see and imagine herself doing the things well that she had previously relied upon her husband to do for her. For example, since her husband always paid the bills, she could now see herself paying the bills easily and on time, and picturing her checkbook or online bank account with plenty of money in it after paying the bills. Ilene can choose to see herself balancing all her accounts or asking for help from someone who is a bookkeeper or accountant until she learns how to do it herself. Either way, she can choose thoughts and feelings that help her feel better. While holding these pictures of herself managing her bills and checkbook well, she can now ask herself:

What can I now think and say to myself to help me feel better yet? I'm learning how to do things I've never done before, and am getting better and better at doing them.

I feel/felt (emotion only): Hopeful (6)

Let's go up another notch:
What can I now think and say to myself to help me feel even better yet? I see myself doing things I had not thought possible before.

I feel Positive Expectation (4)

To feel better yet, what can I now think and say to myself: I am capable of taking care of myself.

I feel (emotion only): Empowered (1)

When you do this process for yourself, it is essential to keep the vibration high so you can feel the energy flow. When energy is flowing, you feel a sensation of opening up, of expansion, of a lightening up throughout your body. You may feel a tingly sensation or a warming sensation. Whatever you feel in your body is fine. With practice you will not only recognize the positive vibes or energy flow, but will also be able to call up the sensation whenever you want. Being in this state of flow is a great time to focus on your vision of the newly reinvented You leading to your truEST life. See it, feel it, believe it, and it is so.

Another exercise to experience energy flow, and which clearly demonstrates to your Logical Left brain hemisphere that energy is real, is an Exercise courtesy of Lynn Grabhorn in Excuse Me, Your Life Is Waiting. Get two straight plastic straws and two wire hangers. (These days you may have to get the hangers at your favorite dry cleaners.) Untwist the hook part of the hanger and using a wire cutter, cut off the hooks of both hangers. Now bend the hangers to form an L. Place the smaller part of the L into each straw. Standing up, hold a straw with a hanger in each hand upright, firmly but not tight enough to feel the wire inside. Bend your elbows so that your upper arms are down by your sides and your lower arms and hands are out in front of you, with the larger part of the wire L facing forward. In this position start to think of thoughts that are of a higher vibration, such as something that makes you smile, and watch what the hangers do. Now think of something that constricts or contracts you, perhaps a recent disagreement or a feeling of being stuck in your old ways, and notice what the hangers do then. You will notice that expansive thoughts and energy vibrations cause the wires to point outward, while constricting thoughts cause the wires to move inward, often to the point of crossing in front of you. Play with this for a while, flipping your thoughts and vibrations back and forth. This works because energy flows where your attention goes, and clearly demonstrates that you are able to change your vibrations and energy flow by changing what you are focusing upon in your mind. While energy is flowing outwardly, enfold your vision of your reinvented self. Be sure that before you stop doing this exercise the last thoughts are ones that cause your energy to flow expansively because you always want to end this exercise on a high vibration.

<u>How Carly reinvented herself by raising her feelings and vibrations</u>: Carly couldn't believe what was happening to her! She and her husband had moved to North Carolina from Arizona for her new job, which she was sure was her dream job. At age 55, she had been so thrilled when she had landed the job as an assistant director in the training division of her new company. But here she was, after only a year, feeling that something was really off with her immediate supervisor. It seemed to her that she was always trying to smooth over ruffled feathers in other departments caused by the actions of her supervisor. Carly was fearful that she would be fired if she didn't support her supervisor, while at the same time believing that the supervisor was making many mistakes. She felt like she was walking on eggshells all the time, but as she was the sole provider for their household, Carly believed that she couldn't just quit her job. Instead, she hired a business coach to help her communicate better with her supervisor. When Carly's supervisor was eventually fired, Carly felt great – she was vindicated and validated. "Things are going to look up now," thought Carly. But instead, Carly's whole world crumbled. Because Carly had been trying to be supportive of her old boss, the

new powers-that-be didn't trust Carly to deal with her colleagues appropriately. However, the company couldn't dismiss Carly without risking a lawsuit since there was no viable cause. Instead, the company continued to pay Carly the same salary, and changed her job duties from those of leadership to those of a "gofer". She was tasked with such things as making photocopies and taking her new director's clothes to the cleaners. It was apparent that the company was trying to get Carly to quit her job, but Carly needed the income! "I'm so depressed," thought Carly. "I can't believe how this dream job has turned into such a nightmare!" Her sense of self-esteem and self-worth had definitely tanked. This was obvious from her physical appearance and demeanor. Previously, Carly had always taken pride in her appearance, and although a bit overweight, always wore stunning outfits and makeup to rival a model's. Now Carly found herself hardly able to get out of bed in the morning. She often came to work without any make-up and her clothes were those she wore around the house. "How could this have happened?" she lamented.

Carly tried in vain to find another position, but not only did she not see any positions that appealed to her, she also felt she would make a piss-poor impression. Carly knew she had to make some internal changes in order to change her external conditions, and consequently decided to work with me. Luckily, Carly was very open to the spiritual principles of the Law of Attraction, so we began working on ways to change her feelings and consequently her vibrations. Carly began to focus on the positives that she had learned from having had the job in the first place. As we worked on changing her vibrations from fear-based to appreciation and gratitude, Carly began to feel hopeful. "Miraculously" Carly began finding positions online that excited her, and for which she applied. Carly was ecstatic when she landed a wonderful job in Florida. She realized she wouldn't have qualified for the new position in Florida if she hadn't had her current job in training. Last I heard from Carly, their house was only on the market for a short time before selling, and she and her husband, Bill, were happily winging it to Orlando!

CHAPTER 9:
STEP FIVE: LISTENING TO OUR BODIES

"I listen with love to my body's messages."

~Louise Hay

A fun experiment that I bet you did as a kid is to stand in the middle of a doorway and press your arms hard against the door frames for a few minutes. After a few minutes of doing this, step out of the doorframe and your arms will automatically float up through no effort of your own. Scientifically, the arm floating has to do with the pressure previously put on your muscles. This next exercise is similar, but done purely with energy flow. Stand with your legs slightly apart and firmly planted on the floor. Have your arms down by your side and relaxed. Now think of something, anything, that you already know raises your vibration. If you are comfortable with calling in the Universe/God/Spirit/Christ Consciousness, do so. While keeping your arms relaxed by your side, you may begin to feel your torso surrounded by an energy field which will begin to lift your arms through no conscious use of your muscles. The higher your arms float, the more energy flow you are experiencing. Recalling how you felt when doing the exercise with the hangers may assist you with this experience as well.

In the 1970's when I first started studying the principles of the Mind/Brain/Body/Spirit being connected, the Western medical community was still doubting the connection, and it wasn't as easy as it is now to find information about the connection. Nowadays this knowledge has gone mainstream, and a lot of the Western medical community currently knows the interconnection that has been known by the Eastern medical community for a long time: The mind and the body are interconnected and it is necessary to treat both to create full health. Louise Hay, in her many works, but especially in her book, Heal Your Body A-Z, has done a wonderful job of specifically delineating what thoughts affect which parts of the body, and how to reverse each of those effects utilizing positive affirmations and visualization. In more general terms, there are three areas of the body most affected by negativity or stress: the head, the back, and the stomach. (When stressed I doubt that you have ever complained of a toe ache!) Headaches are usually the result of negative thinking. When you notice the onset of a headache, think about what you had been thinking about within the last two hours, and I bet you will find the source of the headache to be negative thinking. Backaches have to do with our sense of support; the upper back is said to reflect feelings of being overwhelmed or having a lot of responsibility "resting on our shoulders." The lower back relates to how much support we feel financially and/or emotionally. The third area, which we say to be our stomachs having issues, is actually our guts, which is the seat of our emotions. Notice the common phrases we use to reflect this, like a gut reaction or "It was like being punched in the gut," when we get bad news. It is also where our intuitive hunches reside, and feelings that occur when we are nervous or excited, such as, "I have butterflies in my stomach." Weight is also clearly linked with our thoughts and beliefs. When we feel weighted down by responsibility or are depressed, we often gain weight. Then there are people who simply can't eat when they are anxious, and the pounds just fly off of them until they look almost anorexic. (Sometimes I wish I were one of the latter – just sayin') The books and workshops by Geneen Roth are excellent resources for understanding and changing our subconscious thoughts as they relate to weight.

Meditation to Attune to Your Body

Meditation or Mindfulness techniques are very helpful for tuning into your body. Having experienced the sensation of energy flow, you can now realize that when you tune into your body, your body acts like a barometer, reading how you are feeling emotionally and energetically. One of the benefits of focusing on your body parts and causing them to relax is to get in touch with where your body energy may be stuck. When you feel stress in your body it is due to unwanted thoughts and beliefs, which have created unpleasant feelings, and consequently blocked energy flow. Recalling the computer analogy of your Mind being the Programmer, your Brain being the CPU, and your Body being the Print Out, through a meditative body scan you can get in touch with where your energy is stuck as a result of your thoughts and beliefs. In addition, it is through your body that you experience your feelings, which, as you have learned, is essential for change. Therefore, as you do the exercise below, pay attention to where your body is tight, especially if there are areas where you usually feel the constriction. I know for myself that there are two areas: one is the left side, upper back top shoulder where the shoulder joins my neck. Whenever I realize I have tension there, I know to stop and think about what I had been thinking about in the recent past. Inevitably, I realize and acknowledge that I had been thinking worrisome and upsetting thoughts which caused the constriction. This gives me the opportunity to meditate in order to release the negative energy. If I don't have time to meditate right then, I employ some relaxation techniques, such as taking three deep breaths and visualizing the tightness to be a rope that is knotted; while taking the deep breaths I see the knot in the rope unravel. I may also employ the Thought Cycle and the use of positive affirmations to replace my previously constricting thoughts. The other area of my body where I commonly feel constriction is in my throat.

Again, when I become aware of this feeling, I acknowledge that there is some area in which I am not fully expressing myself, and if I don't have the time or am not in a location where meditation is feasible, I then employ Positive Self-Talk. I usually have a follow-up conversation with the person I didn't share my feelings with earlier. I am happy to say that these occurrences are a lot less frequent and less intense than they used to be prior to my own "reinvention!"

How to Meditate

If you are like many other people, you may be having an "ouch" reaction to the idea of meditation, possibly thinking that it means turning into a pretzel and arduously keeping still for long periods of time. Actually, it is a very simple practice and one that can literally change your life for the better. Consistency is more important than intensity, so start off meditating daily for short periods of time. Sit in a comfortable position with both feet firmly on the floor, and your arms resting comfortably in your lap. The recommended position is to have each hand on its side with fingertips lightly touching so that your thumb and index finger or your thumb and the next two fingers form a circle. If this is uncomfortable for you, that's okay. Just find a position that is comfortable without crossing any of your limbs since that cuts off energy flow. Either close your eyes or lower your eyelids into a soft focus eye gaze and pay attention to your breath. Breathe in with a deep breath from the diaphragm. If you are a singer, you know what this means. If you are like me and can't carry a tune, you may want to practice this. To practice breathing diaphragmatically, place one hand on your upper chest and place the other hand right above your belly button. Inhale through your nostrils only, causing the hand placed on your upper chest to rise first, and then fill up the bottom part of your lungs so that your other hand now is pushed out. Hold your breath for a count of three, and then slowly exhale through your mouth causing the breath to expel from your lower part of your chest first so that your lower hand goes inward and then expel the air in your upper chest causing the upper hand to go inward. Practice this for a few minutes to get comfortable with it. Let go of any concern whether you are doing it exactly right; just do your best to follow the directions and relax. To keep your mind focused, you can count as you breathe in for a count of three, then slowly exhale through your mouth for a count of three or longer. Just focus on your breath and count three times. Breath is a great connection between our bodies and our subconscious mind because it is the only function of the body that is both controllable and automatic. We don't need to think about breathing, but when we want to direct it, we can.

Next in the exercise, focus on each part of your body. Focus your attention on your toes, and relax them completely. Then focus your attention on your feet, and cause the muscles in your feet to relax. Go up your body, to your calves, knees, thighs, pelvis, buttocks, stomach, chest, back, arms, hands, shoulders, neck, jaws, cheeks, eyelids, forehead and scalp, placing each part of your body in a deep state of relaxation as you do so. Take at least one deep breath for each body part upon which you focus. If your mind wanders, just gently bring it back to focus on your body or you can simply focus on counting your breaths.

You will find that the more you practice, the more deeply relaxed you will become and the longer you will be able to be still and enjoy the meditation experience. At first, you may want to set a timer or put an alarm on your phone. If you have never meditated before, just set the timer for a minute, gradually increasing the time span by five minute increments until you can be still for 15-20 minutes. An excellent book to help start a meditation practice is Success through Stillness by Russell Simmons. He goes into the benefits of meditation at length, and then introduces a good way to get started with meditation. According to Simmons, the best word upon which to focus, which has also been termed a mantra, is not Om, as you might expect – I know I did - but Rumm. I also offer a transcript of a more in-depth meditation that works great with or without meditative music. If you would like the transcript, just let me know by emailing me at Trudy@truestlifecoaching.com. You can also check out YouTube for some good meditations online.

Disassociating from Your Emotions

Interestingly, there is another technique that you may want to try when you are experiencing an unpleasant emotion, which is the exact opposite of getting in touch with your body. It is an NLP exercise called the Timeline for Managing Emotions, which I learned from Eben Pagan's Virtual Coach program. Basically, it is a way to disassociate yourself and your body from emotions which can be holding you back from transforming your essential self. First, I want to clarify that all emotions are valuable. They are our guidance system to know what we don't want, or about which we are feeling discontent, and to know what we do want or for which we are longing. Nonetheless, there are times when disassociating from experiencing an emotion, especially if you have learned what you need to learn from that emotion, serves your essential self best. Three emotions you may want to dissociate from are guilt, fear, and anxiety.

Guilt is caused by something from the past that you either wished you had done or something in the past that you wish you hadn't done. Fear is an emotion usually experienced in the present. Again, fear is valuable because it is what allowed the human species to survive. If you are experiencing fear in the present because you are trying to avoid something, the thing you are trying to avoid could be just the thing that can help you reinvent yourself. It might be useful to think of fear as False Evidence Appearing Real. You may need to feel the fear, and do what you fear anyway in order to live your TruEST life. As Neale Donald Walsch, author of the Conversations with God series, says, **"Life begins at the end of your comfort zone."** Think about whether that is what is going on for you or not before deciding to disassociate from the Fear. If, however, disassociating from the emotion of fear helps you take action in the present, this exercise may be very helpful to you. Anxiety is fear about something which may occur in the future. Anxiety can be helpful because it causes you to look at consequences, which may cause you to do something which helps yourself. An example is studying for a licensing exam so that you can start a new career about which you are passionate. However, too much anxiety can cause you to go into prevention mode, thus stopping you from taking the licensing exam. After reading the instructions below, close your eyes to visualize the experience. Because this is an exercise that may be easier to do with someone talking you through it, you can either contact me for support at Trudy@TruestLifeCoaching.com or you can record the script in Appendix G and play it for yourself.

TIMELINE FOR MANAGING EMOTIONS TOOL

You are to create in your mind an imaginary timeline of your life from your birth to your eventual death. You might imagine the past to be behind you, the present to be right where you are, and the future may seem to be in front of you. Or you may imagine that the past is to your left and the future is to your right, or vice-versa. Whichever way works for you is the image to use. For this first time doing this exercise, use events that on a scale of 1-10 only cause a 3-4 in emotional intensity. Now here is the part that would be helpful to have someone read slowly and with feeling to you, or to have recorded it and play it back. Each scenario can take up to 10 minutes:

"See and feel yourself to be at the Now point on the timeline, and consider the situation about which you feel fear. Now visualize another 'you' and have that 'other you' step away from the first you and see the 'other you' getting into a hot air balloon. See yourself rising above the timeline in the hot air balloon, drifting above and away from the first you that is on the Now point of the timeline. How does it feel to be in the hot air balloon? What are the sensations in your body? You may feel a shift in the emotion of fear. Whatever you experience is just right for you. When you are ready, see the hot air balloon with you inside drifting gently back to the Now point on the time line. Get out of the balloon. How do you feel now?"

If you would like to do this exercise regarding any guilt from the past, bring an event to mind about which you felt guilt, again with an intensity of only 3 or 4. Now have the person continue reading:

"Step back into the hot air balloon; you can take both versions of you along if you want, or you may choose to leave one behind. Now float the hot air balloon toward the past on your timeline. As you do, imagine past events going by, until you go past the event that occurred for which you are experiencing guilt. From your viewpoint further in the past than the guilt-event, turn toward the Now point and view that past event. How are you feeling? What are you experiencing in your body? You

may feel a shift in the emotion of guilt. Whatever you experience is just right for you. When you are ready, see the hot air balloon with you inside drifting gently back to the Now point on the time line. Get out of the balloon. How do you feel now?"

Now do the same thing for the feeling of anxiety about an event or situation that may occur in the future:

"Step back into the hot air balloon; you can take both versions of you along if you want, or you may choose to leave one behind. Now float the hot air balloon toward the future on your timeline. As you do so, imagine future events going by, until you go past the event that is to occur in the future about which you are experiencing anxiety. From your viewpoint further in the future than the event, turn toward the Now point and view the future event by looking back. How are you feeling? What are you experiencing in your body? You may feel a shift in the emotion of anxiety. Whatever you experience is just right for you. When you are ready, see the hot air balloon with you inside drifting gently back to the Now point on the time line. Get out of the balloon. How do you feel now?"

<u>My Thoughts/Feelings/Body Connection Stories</u>: I remember back when I was married to my first husband, Rick, and had the Hong Kong flu which I couldn't shake! It was a horrible Chicago winter (I know, aren't most of them?) but this one was bad even for Chicago. My doctor, who had known me since I was 13, prescribed an antibiotic and said I should feel better in 48 hours. After 48 hours came and went, I called him to let him know I was no better. He then prescribed another antibiotic, assuring me that I would feel better, and another 48 hours went by with me continuing to have such a debilitating fever

that I could only get up to go the bathroom. This scenario went on and on for close to six weeks. After about five weeks of this illness, Rick went out of town for a few days, causing me to rely on a neighbor to take out our dog. (We were living in a high rise in a condo that had been mine before our marriage.) To say the least, Rick was not helpful or sympathetic during this long stretched-out illness and I had been thinking about how bad our relationship had become. I was already thinking that if things didn't improve by June (which was our anniversary month) I would ask for a divorce, but in January I still wanted to give our marriage a few more months to try to make it better. When Rick returned from his trip, I was still sick. The tipping point came when he left the next morning and blew off walking the dog for its 6:00 PM walk. When Rick came home at 10:00 PM, I told him to leave (you can mess with me, but not with my dog!). I'm telling you all this so you can appreciate the fact that within 48 hours of telling Rick to leave, my fever broke!

Conversely, in 2002, I had a herniated disk in my back which caused excruciating sciatica pain down my right leg. For ten months I was literally unable to sit down for more than ten minutes at a time. In an effort to avoid back surgery, I worked with a chiropractor, who four years previously had been able to relieve my pain. During this second period of being in constant pain, I had become very depressed, which being in chronic pain can do, along with being unhappy at work and at home. Once again, I had thrown out the spiritual principles I knew, and was not listening to my higher self at all. Reluctantly on my part, surgery was scheduled, but then had to be postponed for six weeks due to me contracting a urinary tract infection. The urinary tract infection turned out to be a blessing in disguise. During the six week interval between the original date of surgery and the second, I "awakened" my true essential self, remembering that being depressed was not a good way to feel when undergoing surgery. I used the six-week postponement to read books that I knew would help, such as Excuse Me, Your Life is Waiting, by Lynn Grabhorn, and Louise Hay's works, resumed meditating and thought-changing. No, I wasn't able to avoid the surgery, but the surgery was highly successful. Shortly after I was wheeled up to my room, I rang for the nurse as instructed, and walked myself into the bathroom. A couple of hours later when I had to ring for the nurse for the same reason, the nurse told me I was the talk of all the nurses on the floor. They were astounded that I was able to get out of bed and walk by myself to the bathroom so soon after surgery. The next day when the surgeon came to see me, he saw the books I was reading on my hospital nightstand, and asked me about them. When I told him the books were about using the power of one's mind to help the body heal, he responded, "Oh, I believe in that!" The surgeon then asked me to walk so that he could see how I was doing. I walked so well that Doc released me that same day instead of the following day, which had been the protocol at the time. After this experience, I vowed to myself to not let conditions, no matter how bad they seemed, ever again take me away from the Truth and Universal principles which I know to be true.

"Prayer and meditation are essential elements of the spiritual life because they focus our thoughts on our Oneness with God and all creation."

~Unity Principle #4

CHAPTER 10: STEP SIX: PUTTING IT TOGETHER BY TAKING ACTION

On Creating Ourselves: ***"The self is not something ready-made, but something in continuous formation through choice of action."***

~John Dewey

This book won't help you create the You you want to become by simply reading about it. Neither does reinventing yourself in order to be your transformed essential self happen by meditating on a mountaintop, contemplating your navel alone. You must take action to experience change. An easy example of this principle is that most of us know that to lose weight we need to eat less and exercise more, but unless we take action, the knowledge alone is insufficient for weight loss. Likewise, going on a diet without doing any internal work is insufficient for any lasting change, as the yo-yo effect of gaining, losing and gaining back weight will attest. We need to work on both our internal as well as our external game to reinvent ourselves. While the exercises learned up until now are necessary parts of the transformation process, they are not sufficient by themselves. It is only by acting on your intuitive guidance and new belief system that you will be able to ultimately change yourself so that you are living a life you love.

"It is not enough to know the Truth; we must put that Truth into action in our lives. We must live the Truth we know."

~Unity Principle #5

However, sometimes you may find yourself in situations in which it is difficult to know what to do or what action to take. It may be difficult to discern whether the small internal voice whispering in your ear is really your intuitive guidance or not. You may wonder if you can trust it, or if it is your old belief system trying to keep you stuck (more on this in Chapter 11 on Obstacles.)

"It is truly said: It does not take much strength to do things, but it requires great strength to decide what to do."

~Chew Ching

Here are some techniques that can really help in your decision – making so that you can take the needed actions.

Meditation:

As you think about or meditate upon what you think would be best for you to do,* think about one decision first. Do you feel contraction or expansion when you imagine choosing that decision?

Next, imagine making the other decision. How do you feel with this decision? Always go for the decision for which you felt the most expansion. The Universe is always working for your good, and therefore, when you feel expansion, know that it is the Universe letting you know what is in your best interest.

Although there were logical reasons for choosing to move to Greensboro, North Carolina, from the Chicago area, when contemplating whether or not to move to Greensboro, I experienced such expansion that despite the objections from my extended family, I just knew it was the right thing for me to do.

Hanger Technique:
Use the straw and hanger technique learned earlier. Contemplate one choice and then another to see how the energy flows. Remember that the decision that is in your best interest will be the one where the energy expands as demonstrated by the wires turning outward.

*Always frame your decision/questions as "Would it be in my best interest to...?" Refrain from stating it as "Should I do this or that?" because the Universe/God has given humankind free will and the power of choice. Consequenty, there are no "shoulds."

As I discussed previously, when back surgery for my herniated disc had to be rescheduled, and I got back to using my spiritual principles, I utilized this hanger technique to keep my energy flowing expansively. As a result, I had no doubts or anxiety going into surgery, which I believe contributed to my healing so quickly and completely.

DBT Wise Mind Technique
Here is a twist on a DBT (Dialectical Behavioral Therapy) counseling technique. According to DBT, we have a Logical Mind and we have an Emotional Mind. There is an intersection between the two Minds where they overlap, which is termed the Wise Mind. The Wise Mind takes both logic and emotion into consideration. To tap into the Wise Mind, make two columns on a piece of paper and in one column write down your pros and in the other column write down your cons of making a particular decision. While writing, use stream of consciousness so that you are brainstorming and not pre-editing yourself. Now on a scale of 1-10, assign an importance value to each pro and to each con, with 10 being the highest. You can have more than one with the same point value. In other words, you are not rank

ordering them. Now add up the points in each column. Which had a higher point value? Using this technique it's possible to have only one or two items in a column and five or six in the other, and the column with the fewest items may still have a higher score. Now here is the twist. Check in with your higher self. Are you happy with the decision that ranked higher? If you are, then that's the decision to make. If you aren't, then your higher self, your intution, your gut, is telling you that despite the logic involved, the other decision is in your highest interest.

I have used this technique with many clients with whom I have worked, and it has helped them make very important decisions, such as whether or not to leave a marriage or to take a new job offer. Inevitably after using this technique, my clients feel relieved at knowing what decision to make.

Musle Testing

Muscle testing or applied kinesiology is a way to get in touch with your subconscious mind to make decisions about what is best for you. According to Energy Therapist, Amy B. Scher, the body has within it and surrounding it an electrical network or grid, which is pure energy. Because energy runs through the muscles in your body, if anything that impacts your electrical system does not maintain or enhance your body's balance, your muscles will virtually "short circuit" or weaken temporarily. Things that might have an impact on your electrical system are thoughts and emotions, foods, and other substances. Using your muscles, you can find what events or emotions "weaken" or "strengthen" your body, thus tapping into your subconscious mind, which really does know what is in your best interest.

The muscle testing technique with which I am the most familiar is to stand with your feet firmly planted and your strongest arm raised from the shoulder straight out to the side, parallel to the floor. Have a partner "test" you as a control measure by asking something that you already know is true, such as your name, after which using his or her two fingers, your partner presses down on your arm, close to but not on your wrist, saying "Resist me." Your partner will feel and judge the strength with which your arm resists being pushed down. Then have your partner ask you something that both of you know is not true, and repeat the process. Untruths always weaken the body system, so your arm will weaken.

After testing your strength in this way, to use muscle testing for decision-making, write down different decisions on pieces of paper, fold the pieces of paper and have your partner label the outside of the papers as 1, 2, 3, etc. One at a time, hold each folded slip of paper next to your chest with your opposite hand, and have your partner test your arm strength as previously described. The partner asks if it's in your best interest to do #1, # 2 or #3, etc. without you knowing what is written on each slip. If there are several questions asked, be sure that your partner records his or her impression of your arm strength after each time so that you will be able to determine which answer gave you the most strength. There is now a lot of research and study backing up the veracity of muscle testing as a way to determine what works best for someone. I used this technique to determine whether writing this book and spending the money to get it published were in my best interest, along with the technique described below. (I wanted to be doubly certain !)

The Sign Technique

There are different ways to do this technique, but here is the way I have been doing it for years, and it has always worked for me! While meditating or just thinking about a decision, tell yourself "If doing X is in my best interest, I will see or hear a _____ within the next 24 (or 48 – whichever feels best) hours. You fill in the blank with whatever comes to mind. It is usually an object or word of some kind. Be sure to note the time you did the technique so that you will know if you saw the sign within the allotted time period. Realizing that a coincidence is just God/the Universe working anonymously, whatever sign you ask for is the correct one, whether you see it or not.

As mentioned above, I also used this technique to decide whether writing this book was in my best interest and I guess you know what the answer was! The sign I used in making that decision was seeing a White Feather since it was a symbol of The Author Incubator, the company I decided to work with to help me write this book. As I was walking into a Pier One store to shop, I saw a set of wine glasses with – yep – a white feather painted on each of them. At other times, I have used whatever pops into mind, knowing that there are no coincidences to what that symbol will be. For example, I was driving (yes, you can do this on the "fly," so to speak) and wanted to know whether or not something my daughter was doing was in her highest and best interest. For some (unknown-to-me) reason, "giraffe" popped into my head. I had been driving because I was on my way to visit someone in their home for the first time, and as I walked into her livingroom, what was on her end table, but – you guessed it – a sculpture of a giraffe. My concern about my daughter was alleviated immediately at this sight.

<u>Beth's Story on Using the Sign Technique</u>: Beth had been so excited to buy her new house; it was just what she wanted after a long and diligent search! The bank had already approved her and she was just waiting for the closing date. A week before the closing date, Beth was informed that her job at a non-profit was ending because the grant for her program at the agency hadn't been re-newed. Beth sat in her supervisor's office crying, not only because of the loss of the job, but also because she thought she would have to give up her house. Beth did the logical thing and contacted her financial advisor who assured her that she would be okay to get the house and pay the mortgage for a few months until she found another job. Nevertheless, Beth was still anxious about moving ahead. She decided to do the sign technique, which she had previously learned from me. Because the house had yellow walls and blue countertops in the kitchen, what popped into Beth's mind was seeing something with yellow and blue together. She was driving at the time she had asked for the sign, and within minutes a school bus painted not only yellow but also blue for the school's colors drove by her! Beth was elated that she had seen her sign, but still had some doubt because, logically, she remained concerned about paying the mortgage without knowing she had a job. So Beth did another sign technique asking for verification that she would soon get a job and that there would not be an issue with paying the mortgage. This time, the idea of an elf popped into her mind. Later that night while thumbing through a magazine, Beth saw not only one but two elves! Beth was finally at ease and went ahead with getting the house. Within a month she had secured another job, and was extremely happy that she had followed her inner guidance.

Some clients with whom I have worked use the same symbol whenever they ask for a sign. I recall my client, Helen, saying she uses the sign of a red cardinal no matter what question she is contemplating. Sometimes, you may hear your "sign" such as in lyrics to a song, or see the "sign" spelled out. One person with whom I worked used the sign "blue bird" and a taxi from the Blue Bird company pulled up! I really like this technique because there is no ambiguity. You either see or hear the sign or you don't within the allotted time period.

The purpose of any of these techniques is to ensure that the actions you decide to take are in service of reinventing yourself in order to live your truEST life. Remember that not taking action is also making a choice; while it may keep you safe, not acting is the same as not growing. Not growing is like dying. After all, remember what "they" say about the road to hell being paved with good intentions!

CHAPTER 11: OBSTACLES TO REINVENTING OURSELVES

"Know that everything, absolutely everything, even when it doesn't appear to be, is working for your highest good."

~Abraham

When my bathroom was recently remodeled, the contractor was not expecting that there would be rotten wood that had to be removed first, but there was, which delayed the process and cost more. Nevertheless, the project was still completed (and looks beautiful, by the way). Knowing that there will be unexpected obstacles that will get in the way of moving forward to your new way of being can be very helpful to countering them. Your ego, or old way of being, is very comfortable with the way things are and has a strong hold on your belief system. To change means the ego has to let go of its old way of being and it will fight your desire to change as if it were fighting for its life, which, in a way, it is! That's because your old self has to "die" in order for your newly reinvented self to be created, just as the old rotten wood in my bathroom had to be removed. No one likes the thought of "dying," so expect that there will be push back to your predictable way of doing things and comfort zone. Your old self, or ego, will try all sorts of tricks, such as causing fear and doubt. Be sure to thank the ego for doing its job of trying to keep you safe and let it know that while you appreciate it, you are in control and are moving forward. If doubt or fear continue to come up, use the various exercises taught in this book, like Self-Talk, Positive Affirmations, and Words to Reprogram to help shift your thinking and beliefs to those of empowerment. Working with Abraham's Emotional Guidance Scale can also raise your vibrations to get you out of those lower level vibes of doubt and fear.

"When she transformed into a butterfly, the caterpillars spoke not of her beauty, but of her weirdness. They wanted her to change back into what she always had been. But she had wings."

~Author Unknown

People in your life will also want to push you back into your old way of being. That is how they know you and how they know to interact with you. You may think that instead of people in your life pulling you down that you can bring them up to your new level of being, and for that matter, I would love it if you encouraged them to get this book! Nonetheless, trust me, it is easier for them to pull you down than for you to pull them up, especially if they are not yet into transformational work. Imagine that you are standing on a chair and an old friend or a family member is standing on the floor next to you. Taking one another's hand, do you think it would be easier for you to pull that individual up onto the chair with you or for the individual on the floor to pull you off the chair and onto the floor? I'm sure you get the point. If people are open to hearing about your new ways of thinking and being, celebrate with them. If not, you may need to employ the Letting in the Good; Letting Out the Bad Exercise taught later in this chapter.

Likewise, there is a theory in the practice of social work called Systems Theory. It is premised on the idea that an effective system is based on individual needs, rewards, expectations, and attributes of the people living in the system. According to this theory, families, couples, and organization members are directly involved in creating and resolving a problem – even if it is an individual issue. Consequently, the impact of change on all parts of the system needs to be considered. Just as it is difficult for an individual to change and maintain that change, it is difficult for the system in which the individual lives and works to allow the change. Members of the system, especially one's family members, will create challenges to your new way of being, especially if part of reinventing yourself is to establish healthy boundaries.

A Truth that I particularly like to hold onto when confronted with external obstacles is the one by Abraham quoted at the start of this chapter: "Know that everything is working for your highest good." There are no exceptions to this Principle, just as there are no exceptions to the Law of Gravity. Recognize, therefore, that things which may seem like obstacles are serving a higher purpose for you. As Colin Tipping in Radical Forgiveness decrees, **"What if there is nothing wrong?"**

The Importance of Self-Care:

"And don't forget to love yourself. You deserve it. You are a gift."

~Louise Hay and David Kessler,
You Can Heal Your Heart

For women, establishing healthy boundaries can be especially difficult because women mistakenly think it is selfish to take care of themselves. A boundary is defined as a limit or line over which you will not allow anyone to cross because of the negative impact on you of its being crossed. Boundaries are an established set of limits over your physical and emotional well-being which you expect others to respect in their relationship with you; the emotional and physical space you need in order to be the real you, your essential self, without pressure from others to be something that you are not. Look again at the chapter on Beliefs, Chapter 7, to see if you may have been, at least up until now, carrying a belief that holds you back from establishing boundaries. That will be true especially if you had circled any of the following beliefs:

#1 Everyone must love me. (It is an absolute necessity that I have love and approval from peers, family, and friends: I am wrong or bad if they don't love or approve of me.)

#12 I must get along with everyone because I couldn't stand it if I hurt someone. (Self-sacrifice is necessary because my needs and wants are not as important as keeping the peace.)

#13 I know that good relationships are based on mutual sacrifice and focus on giving. (I must constantly deny myself because it is better to give than to receive.)

#14 I can't express my real self or my needs. (I have to please others no matter what the cost so that I will not be abandoned or rejected.)

Creating a new set of beliefs for these issues will be paramount in reinventing yourself. In fact, these are the exact beliefs I needed to change in order to leave Illinois as well as to leave my marriage with Ray. If necessary, re-read Chapter 7 to help you establish beliefs that will help with self-care and boundary-setting. You may also need to use Positive Affirmations regarding self-worth that were given to you in Chapter 6 to help with this. I believe that there is such a thing as healthy selfishness. Remember that flight attendants tell passengers to put their own oxygen masks on first before helping others! You cannot help others unless you take care of yourself first.

According to Bart McCormick, MSW, LCSW, "Self-denying is when we deny that we have our own wishes, preferences and needs to other people – and sometimes even to ourselves. This makes it hard for others around us to...consider and respect our needs and wishes (since we haven't let them know what they are). This is a special case of self-depriving behavior, and usually results from either a fear of being selfish or a fear others won't respect or consider our needs and wishes if we express them." If this sounds familiar to you, it's time to work on it with Self-Talk and Changing One's Belief, or by raising your emotional vibration as discussed in Chapter 8 on Feelings and Vibes. Self-care is necessary for you to live your truEST life. McCormick further defines self-care as "the name we use to describe a healthy and balanced approach to responding to the wants and needs of others *and* ourselves…Self-care also means that we recognize that we need to put our needs before the needs and wants of others at times, and to do so without guilt and unfair self-accusations of selfishness…the decisions involved in self-care are not always clear-cut or easy, and self-care is more like an art we (hopefully!) learned to do more effectively over time."

Jackie's Story on Setting Boundaries: Jackie is a very capable professional woman, who holds a good part-time job, is raising her son, and has gone back to grad school. She is quite accomplished and does well in her job. Nonetheless, Jackie has always had difficulty standing up for herself with her family members. While she could express her opinions at work, Jackie was immobilized by fear to do so with her family, especially with her sister who had been diagnosed as bi-polar. Since early childhood, Jackie's immediate family system had structured itself around keeping Jackie's sister calm, which meant doing whatever the sister wanted. When Jackie first started working with me, she struggled with the way her sister would take things over when visiting Jackie's home, including Jackie's infant son, even though the sister did not have any children of her own. As Jackie became better at establishing healthy boundaries, she started interacting differently with first her father (whom she felt was the easier parent), then after some two steps forward and one step back experiences, with her mother, and finally with her sister. Although her sister has not been happy with her new inability to control Jackie and has consequently created discord within the family, Jackie has been able to set and hold the limits of the boundaries she has established regarding how her sister interacts with her, her husband, and their son. (For example, the sister can no longer drop by unexpectedly.) As a matter of fact, Jackie is now working on standing up for herself with her husband. While this has caused some domestic squabbles, Jackie is feeling better about herself and her ability to be a good mother and role model for her son.

Remember that obstacles from others have to do with them, not you, as well as their desire to keep things the same. Others may be frightened by your growth and what it may mean for your relationship. However, people who truly love you will encourage your essential-self transformation because they will want what is best for you. For example, my sister, Sharon, was not happy when I moved away from Chicago to Greensboro. However, my sister and my Chicagoland friends have become very supportive of my decision after witnessing how happy I am in my current life.

If you're concerned whether a decision you need to make is in your best interest *as well as someone else's,* use one of the techniques on decision-making that you learned about in the last chapter. You may also find this simple exercise below useful:

LETTING IN THE GOOD; LETTING OUT THE BAD TOOL

After each of the following questions ask yourself "What Needs to Stay In?" and "What Needs to Go Out?" and write your answers down.

Actually writing down your answers rather than keeping your answers in your head will give you more clarity.

With People and Relationships: "Do they have a positive influence on my life?"

With Emotions and Thoughts: "Am I taking ownership of my emotions and thoughts or am I blaming others?" (Words to Reprogram given in Chapter 6 can help you with this one.)

With Habits and Behaviors: Are they beneficial for my well-being and health?

You may find that doing this exercise is pretty scary, especially the first question about people and relationships. Sometimes the healthiest thing for yourself is to let go of some people and relationships, and realizing that letting them go may be the best way for you to promote self-care, which is what I concluded when I left Ray. It wasn't an easy decision, but I knew I couldn't live my truEST life unless I did so. If you are not good to yourself, no one else will be either.

Fear of Failure is often an internal obstacle to reinventing yourself. If you circled Belief #2 in the Limiting Beliefs Exercise, "I must be good at everything. (I must be unfailingly competent and almost perfect in all that I undertake) then Fear of Failure is a belief that you have held, at least up until now. In addition to changing the wording on this belief, as instructed previously, a helpful reframe can also be to think of Babe Ruth, the great baseball player, or Thomas Edison, the inventor of the lightbulb, among other great inventions. At the time Babe Ruth held the record for the most homeruns, he also held the record for the most strikeouts. It took Edison more than 10,000 tries before he was able to successfully create the electric lightbulb. Right before his success, Edison was asked if he wasn't tired of failing. Edison replied, "I have not failed. I've just found 10,000 ways that won't work." Another thing you may want to do to conquer this fear is to post positive quotes from outliers where you can see them daily. Three quotes that I particularly like are:

"There is only one thing that makes a dream impossible to achieve: the fear of failure."

~Paulo Coelho

"Everything you want is on the other side of fear."

~Jack Canfield

"Every adversity, every failure, every heartache carries with it the seed of an equal or greater benefit."

~Napoleon Hill

If you decide to use these positive affirmations/quotes or any others, be sure to follow the instructions presented earlier on Positive Affirmations and hand print them out.

One of my favorite examples of reinventing oneself is the Mama pig, Rosita, in the movie "Sing," who reinvented herself from a housewife toiling with drudgery to a wonderful singer and star. (By the way, if you haven't seen the movie, I highly recommend it. Your vibrations will definitely be high after seeing it!) In the movie, "Trolls," Princess Poppy shows extreme bravery in rescuing her friends against all odds. On her way through the scary forest she sings, "Hey, I'm not giving up today – There is nothing in my way – And if you knock me over – I will get back up again." "Failure, the greatest teacher it is," declared Yoda to Luke Skywalker in "The Last Jedi" movie. (By the way, can you tell I have young grand-children?)

In sum, obstacles may come from within yourself in the form of thoughts, limiting beliefs, or from lower vibrational feelings – or the obstacles may come from others close to you. To be your newly reinvented self, I suggest that you decide to see any obstacles on your path to living your truEST life as just hills to get over, and keep moving forward. Whether you decide to move forward with your new truEST life path or allow the obstacles to deter you, is your choice, my friend.

You may also find that a good coach can especially assist you in overcoming these obstacles to keeping you on course to your truEST life.

As always, if I can be of assistance, please contact me at;

Trudy@TruestLifeCoaching.com or call 336-763-4611.

CHAPTER 12: COMPLETING THE INSTRUCTIONAL (WO)MANUAL TO REINVENT YOURSELF

"It's time to begin righting the story of your life."

~David Jeremiah

You now have the parts and the tools to reinvent yourself. Here is a "parts list" and instructional summary of each for easy reference:

Instructional Schematic

Desire: In this (Wo)manual, you have learned that for positive change to occur and for you to be willing to reinvent yourself so that you can live your truEST life, you first have to have a strong desire. Your desire to get out of your comfort zone has to be stronger than your wish to play it safe. Your desire to move toward your longing or pleasure needs to be stronger than your pain or fear of changing, and you now have tools to help you keep your desire strong. Use them often. In using the tools, remember to focus on your desire by thinking only about what you want instead of what you don't want, because your *at*tention is much more important than your *in*tention.

Expectancy/Vision: You now know the necessity of having a clear positive vision of what you want along with experiencing feelings that the desired vision/result ***has already occurred*** in order to reinvent yourself. You know that to live from your vision you have to act as if you are already the actualized, truEST self in your vision. Keep this vision in front of you at all times. Have it written out, make a vision board, and look and think about your vision throughout the day; see it and feel the feelings as if your vision has already manifested. One client has reminders on her cell phone which ding periodically throughout the day to remind her to stop whatever she is doing and see herself within her actualized vision.

Belief/Faith: In addition, you have learned the importance of having Belief, or Faith that change ***can*** occur. You now know ways to strengthen your Belief (faith) in yourself with your Vision as your guide. Strengthen your Belief by meditating or visualizing daily, seeing yourself as your fully expanded, expressed, reinvented self living your truEST life.

Tools to Reprogram Your Mind, Brain, Body and Spirit

Thoughts: After assembling the tools of Desire, Belief and Expectancy or Vision together, the first step in the reinvention process is to change your thoughts. You have the power to stop any limiting thought from gathering energy and impacting your reality by employing the Thought Cycle. Once aware of a negative or limiting thought, stop it, and replace it with a positive or expansive thought. I suggest using Words to Reprogram and the Self-Talk Exercise regularly. This helps you respond rather than react to events in your life because, as you now know, events in your life do not cause you to feel any unpleasant emotion, such as anger or fear, but rather your thoughts about the events create those feelings. You now have the power tools and the ability to change those thoughts.

Limitless beliefs: You now know that just believing something is true doesn't mean that it is. You are aware of what your limiting – small b – beliefs are and know that you have the power and ability to change them to limitless ones. With your Vision as your guide, you can utilize your Mind, Brain, Body and Spirit to reprogram your thoughts and thereby your beliefs because changing your thoughts changes your beliefs, which are merely coalesced thoughts. Positive affirmations using Words to Reprogram are especially helpful with this. By changing your beliefs you know how to reframe your diagram (story) and free up energy to reinvent a whole new way of being and creating a life you love. Tweaking a quote by Goethe remember that, "*(Wo)*man is made by *her* belief. As *s*he believes, so *s*he is." (Italics mine)

Feelings and Vibrations: As your beliefs and thoughts change, your feelings change. As the (Wo)manual instructs, our feelings raise or lower our vibrations. Use either of the Emotional Scales as tools to up your vibrations bit by bit. You can also up your vibrations by playing around with your energy fields, such as using the straw with hangers technique, or doing something physical to change your state of being. Remember to smile, fist pump, or dance to happy music!

Self-Care: Positive self-care is the hallmark of being your truEST self. Take good care of yourself by surrounding yourself with positive books, movies, activities and especially with people who will support your growth. As Abraham proclaimed in The Law of Attraction by Esther and Jerry Hicks, ***"What is important is that I am pleased with me, and as I see myself, I certainly am."***

Getting a coach could be one of the most important things you can do for self-care because, as the old L'Oréal haircare commercials used to say, "I am worth it!" Get recommendations for one from someone you know, or contact me at Trudy@TruestLifeCoaching.com.

Final Instructions for Putting Together Your Reinvented Self:
"Human beings by changing the inner attitudes of their minds, can change the outer aspects of their lives."

~William James

In sum, to reinvent yourself and live your truEST life, it is first necessary to change your thoughts; change your thoughts to change your beliefs; change your beliefs to change your feelings; change your feelings to change your vibrations. Higher vibrations will then support you in appropriate self-care. You'll just know what to do to best take care of yourself because those things will feel joyful and expansive as they will be in alignment with your vibrations. Once your inner game has become thus empowered and successfully transformed, by Universal Law your outer world will have to reflect those changes, drawing into your world opportunities, events and people that align with your vision of your truEST self and life.

However, there is one more very important tool that must be used in order to complete your Vision or the inner movie of your reinvented self and life. Since you are the Hollywood director of your life, it is now time for "Lights, camera, and... **Action!** You must take action to manifest your truEST life, because, to quote Joel A. Barker,

"Vision without action is merely a dream. Action without vision just passes the time. Vision with action can change the world."

To change your world (life), take actions that are in alignment with the newly invented essential-self transformed YOU. Using your Vision, move forward to create the life you envision, walking (maybe even skipping!) along your truEST life path filled with health, love, happiness, peace, and abundance! Use the tools of Meditation, Muscle Testing and Wise Mind to know what decisions and actions to take.

CAUTION: But beware of the "Caution" Signs that may arise, such as fear and doubt, also known as Obstacles.

Be prepared for the obstacles that may come up to thwart you from moving along your path of your truEST life ! Obstacles can be internal, such as a fear of failure or doubting your abilities to succeed. They can also be external, such as push-back from family or friends. Instead of putting on your "safety goggles," put on your "psychic shield" goggles to counter obstacles and keep them from affecting you. Put up positive quotes from outliers where you can see them. Utilize the Thought Cycle with positive affirmations, or reframe your Self-Talk whenever necessary to refute any remaining limiting beliefs. If necessary, review the instructions on using the tools presented earlier in this (Wo)manual, or call or email me.

One more empowering tool to use to eliminate obstacles is to focus on Unity Principle #1:

"There is only one ultimate power in the Universe. That power is God and its nature is absolute, unchanging good."

THANK YOU FOR USING THIS INSTRUCTIONAL (WO)MANUAL TO REINVENT YOURSELF:

"Remember, you are only one decision away from a totally different life."

~Author unknown

You really are only one decision away from a totally different life. The decision is yours and yours alone. You can make your life into a winning game, no matter what conditions seem like, or you can put this book on the bookshelf or turn off the e-reader and stay in your comfort zone. As Tony Robbins tells us, ***"If you do what you've always done, you'll get what you've always gotten."***

While the ideas, concepts, tools and techniques presented in this (Wo)manual are actually very simple, simple doesn't necessarily mean easy to incorporate into your life. Making changes, even positive ones, can be daunting – if you let it. Consequently, many people have found that having support, such as a transitions coach like myself, or joining a group of like-minded women who are also reinventing themselves, can be very beneficial.

As you continue down your truEST life path, I'd love to hear how it's going for you. Please let me know what has worked, with any questions you may have, or if I can be of further help to you along your truEST life journey. As a thank you gift, you can also download a helpful free assessment tailored just for YOU. This assessment will help you determine the best first steps for YOU to take to reinvent yourself.

Thank you, again, for taking this journey down your truEST life path to reinventing yourself with me. Whether by yourself or with support, I know you can do it!

Contact me at Trudy@TruestLifeCoaching.com or call 336-763-4611 if I can be of help or service in any way.

Sincerely,
Trudy R. Tobias, MSW, LCSW
Therapist and Life Coach
TruEST Life Coaching and Counseling

(WO)MANUAL INSTRUCTION TOOLS

Note: The techniques and tools presented are like birth control: They only work when you use them consistently and persistently!

APPENDIX A: VISION TOOL

If you would like some help in creating your vision, you can use the following as a template:

Physically, I am healthy with a strong immune system, and

Thank you, God. (or Universe or Great Spirit, whatever works for you.)

Emotionally, I am stable and

Thank you, God. (or Universe or Great Spirit, whatever works for you.)

Mentally, I have a positive outlook and

Thank you, God. (or Universe or Great Spirit, whatever works for you.)

Spiritually, I am growing in the virtues of faith, intuition, hope and love

____

____

____

Thank you, God. (or Universe or Great Spirit, whatever works for you.)

I am enjoying my relationship/s with

____

____

____

I am loving these relationships because they are uplifting and supportive and

____

____

____

Thank you, God. (or Universe or Great Spirit, whatever works for you.)

I am enjoying and loving my relationship with myself. I know I am worthy and

____

____

____

Thank you, God. (or Universe or Great Spirit, whatever works for you.)

I am enjoying the work that I do. I am now

____

____

____

____

____

Thank you, God. (or Universe or Great Spirit, whatever works for you.)

I am loving how my work helps me serve the world by

____

____

____

____

____

Thank you, God. (or Universe or Great Spirit, whatever works for you.)

I am fulfilled by my hobbies and interests, and love having the time and money to do them. I am having so much fun with/by doing

____

____

____

____

____

Thank you, God. (or Universe or Great Spirit, whatever works for you.)

I am earning $__________ (be specific here) annually. I am loving the time and money freedom that earning this income affords me. As a result of this income, I am now able to spend my time

____

____

____

Thank you, God. (or Universe or Great Spirit, whatever works for you.)

I am enjoying the environment I have created at work and at home. I am loving that my space is

____

____

____

Thank you, God. (or Universe or Great Spirit, whatever works for you.)

APPENDIX B: WORDS TO REPROGRAM TOOL

COMMANDS

WORDS AND PHRASES TO USE	WORDS AND PHRASES TO CANCEL
I prefer...	Should (not)
I want...	Must
I would like it if...	Ought to, Have to

OVER-GENERALIZATIONS

WORDS AND PHRASES TO USE	WORDS AND PHRASES TO CANCEL
Sometimes	Always
A lot	Never
Often	No one, None
Some people	Everyone, All

RESPONSIBILITY

WORDS AND PHRASES TO USE	WORDS AND PHRASES TO CANCEL
I am responsible for...	You make me ______ (i.e., angry, sick)
I chose to feel...	It's so-and-so's fault, not mine
I made myself feel...	That makes me_____ (i.e., angry, sick)

CATASTROPHIZING

WORDS AND PHRASES TO USE	WORDS AND PHRASES TO CANCEL
I can handle it	The worst
It's OK to make mistakes	Horrible
It's OK to...	Terrible
I would prefer___, and it's OK if...	Unfair, Impossible, Can't

APPENDIX C: SELF-TALK TOOL

Event, stated factually:

What did I say/think to myself when this event occurred?

I feel/felt (emotion only):

Because:

LIST OF EMOTIONS

Amazed, Angry, Annoyed, Anxious, Ashamed, Bitter, Bored, Comfortable, Confused, Content, Depressed, Determined, Disdainful, Disgusted, Eager, Embarrassed, Energetic, Envious, Excited, Foolish, Furious, Frustrated, Grieving, Happy, Hopeful, Hurt, Inadequate, Insecure, Irritated, Inspired, Joyful, Lonely, Lost, Jealous, Loving, Miserable, Motivated, Nervous, Overwhelmed, Peaceful, Proud, Relieved, Resentful, Sad, Satisfied, Scared, Self-conscious, Shocked, Silly, Stupid, Suspicious, Tense, Terrified, Trapped, Uncomfortable, Worried, Worthless

APPENDIX D: POSITIVE AFFIRMATIONS TOOL

POSITIVE AFFIRMATIONS ON ACCEPTANCE

- Each day I do the best that I can; it is enough to have done my best
- I accept who I am
- Even though I have had negative experiences in the past, I am still a good person
- I've already been through other painful experiences, and I survived
- This, too, shall pass
- Although my feelings make me uncomfortable right now, I can accept them
- I can be anxious and still deal with the situation
- This is an opportunity for me to learn how to cope with my feelings/fears
- My anxiety/fear/sadness/anger won't kill me; it just doesn't feel good right now
- It's okay to feel sad/anxious/afraid/angry sometimes
- I deserve to be happy
- I deserve to be loved

POSITIVE AFFIRMATIONS ON CHOICE AND CHANGE

- I have the power to change myself
- I can make my own choices and decisions
- I am free to choose to live as I wish and to give priority to my desires
- I can choose happiness whenever I wish, no matter what my circumstances

- I am flexible and open to change in every aspect of my life
- My thoughts don't control my life; I do
- I can think different thoughts if I want to
- I'm not in danger right now
- I'm strong and I can deal with this
- I care about myself and other people
- I act with confidence
- I love myself

POSITIVE AFFIRMATIONS ON MY PURPOSE

- I'm here for a reason
- There's a purpose to my life, even though I might not always see it

*Various affirmations taken from The Dialectical Behavior Therapy Skills Workbook by Marsha Linehan, and from The Relaxation and Stress Management Workbook by McKay, Davis & Fanning

APPENDIX E: LIMITING BELIEFS TOOL

1. Everyone must love me. (It is an absolute necessity that I have love and approval from peers, family, and friends: I am wrong or bad if they don't love or approve of me.)
2. I must be good at everything. (I must be unfailingly competent and almost perfect in all that I undertake.) Note: Perfectionists will resonate with this one.
3. When people don't do what they should, they should get what's coming to them. (Certain people are evil, wicked and villainous, and should be punished.)
4. Things should be different. (It is horrible when people and things are not the way I want them to be; there is only one good or right way to do something – my way!)
5. It's your fault I feel this way. (Naturally, external events cause me to react the way I do.)
6. I know something bad will happen. (I feel fear or anxiety about anything that is unknown, uncertain, or potentially dangerous.)
7. It's easier not to try. (It is easier to avoid life's problems than to face life's difficulties and responsibilities.) If you have circled this belief, please add your standard excuses to avoid responsibility here:

   ____

   ____

   ____

8. I need someone stronger than I am. (I can't make independent judgments or express my needs without relying on someone smarter/in authority, etc.)

9. I can't help being this way; I can't change. (Because of what happened in my past, it is natural for me to be the way I am and there's nothing I can do about it.)
10. I am such a good person that your problem is my problem. (I take responsibility for other people's problems, especially people I care about. I would be selfish otherwise.) Note: Moms, in particular, may get sucked into this one.
11. I am helpless and have no control over what I feel. (i.e., Of course, I am depressed and anxious; I can't help it.)
12. I must get along with everyone because I couldn't stand it if I hurt someone. (Self-sacrifice is necessary because my needs and wants are not as important as keeping the peace.)
13. I know that good relationships are based on mutual sacrifice and focus on giving. (I must constantly deny myself because it is better to give than to receive.)
14. I can't express my real self or my needs. (I have to please others no matter what the cost so that I will not be abandoned or rejected.)
15. Being alone is horrible. (I cannot be happy, have pleasure or be fulfilled when/if I am alone.)
16. I cannot be happy unless I have the perfect relationship with someone who loves me.
17. Life is not fair because X happened to me. I should never feel pain; I am entitled to a good life.
18. My worth depends on how much I have achieved and produced.
19. I should never feel anger because it is automatically bad and destructive.
20. If I am selfish in any way, I am bad or wrong.
21. I don't have to express myself or communicate because that person (my spouse, partner, child, good friend, etc.) should

know what I am thinking. (I know what they think because I know them so well and they should know what I am thinking, too.)

22. Everyone else is doing so much better than I am. (I see only the good and positive aspects in others and when I compare myself to them, I don't measure up.) Note: Social media helps perpetuate this belief because we start to compare our insides with everyone else's outsides.
23. Because X happened, I must be a bad, worthless, or underserving person. (I must be a bad person because something painful happened to me.) Note: Annalise was stuck here.

APPENDIX F: EMOTIONAL SCALE FOR YOUR TRUEST LIFE TOOL

Glad

1. Joy/Appreciation/Empowered/Freedom/Love
2. Passion
3. Enthusiasm/Eagerness/Happiness
4. Positive Expectation/Belief
5. Optimism
6. Hopefulness
7. Contentment

Sad

8. Boredom
9. Pessimism
12. Disappointment
16. Discouragement
21. Guilt/Unworthiness
22. Grief/Depression/Despair/Powerlessness

Mad

10. Frustration/Irritation/Impatience
11. Overwhelmed
15. Blame
17. Anger
18. Revenge
19. Hatred/Rage
20. Jealousy

Afraid

13. Doubt
14. Worry
21. Insecurity
22. Fear

APPENDIX G: IMAGINARY TIMELINE SCRIPT TO DISOCCIATE EMOTIONS TOOL

Directions: You are to create in your mind an imaginary timeline of your life from your birth to your eventual death. You might imagine the past to be behind you, the present right where you are, and the future may seem to be in front of you. Or you may imagine that the past is to your left and the future is to your right, or vice-versa. Whichever way works for you is the image to use. For this first time doing this exercise, use events that on a scale of 1-10 only cause a 3-4 in emotional intensity. Now here is the part that would be helpful to have someone read slowly and with feeling to you. Each scenario can take up to 10 minutes:

"See and feel yourself to be at the Now point on the timeline, and consider the situation about which you feel fear. Now visualize another 'you' and have that 'other you' step away from the first you and see the 'other you' getting into a hot air balloon. See yourself rising above the timeline in the hot air balloon, drifting above and away from the first you that is on the Now point of the timeline. How does it feel to be in the hot air balloon? What are the sensations in your body? You may feel a shift in the emotion of fear. Whatever you experience is just right for you. When you are ready, see the hot air balloon with you inside drifting gently back to the Now point on the time line. Get out of the balloon. How do you feel now?"

"Step back into the hot air balloon; you can take both versions of you along if you want, or you may choose to leave one behind. Now float the hot air balloon toward the past on your timeline. As you do, imagine

past events going by, until you go past the event that occurred for which you are experiencing guilt. From your viewpoint further in the past than the guilt-event, turn towards the Now point and view that past event. How are you feeling? What are you experiencing in your body? You may feel a shift in the emotion of guilt. Whatever you experience is just right for you. When you are ready, see the hot air balloon with you inside drifting gently back to the Now point on the time line. Get out of the balloon. How do you feel now?"

"Step back into the hot air balloon; you can take both versions of you along if you want, or you may choose to leave one behind. Now float the hot air balloon toward the future on your timeline. As you do so, imagine future events going by, until you go past the event that is to occur in the future about which you are experiencing anxiety. From your viewpoint further in the future than the event, turn towards the Now point and view the future event by looking back. How are you feeling? What are you experiencing in your body? You may feel a shift in the emotion of anxiety. Whatever you experience is just right for you. When you are ready, see the hot air balloon with you inside drifting gently back to the Now point on the time line. Get out of the balloon. How do you feel now?"

From Eben Pagan,
Virtual Coach Progam

APPENDIX H: LETTING IN THE GOOD; LETTING OUT THE BAD TOOL

After each of the following questions ask yourself "What Needs to Stay In?" and "What Needs to Go Out?" and write your answers down. Actually writing down your answers rather than keeping your answers in your head will give you more clarity.

With People and Relationships: "Do they have a positive influence on my life?"

With Emotions and Thoughts: "Am I taking ownership of my emotions and thoughts or am I blaming others?" (Words to Reprogram given in Chapter 6 can help you with this one.)

With Habits and Behaviors: Are they beneficial for my well-being and health?

FURTHER READING

Ask and It Is Given, by Esther and Jerry Hicks (Abraham), Hay House, 2007

Excuse Me, Your Life Is Waiting, by Lynn Grabhorn, Hara Publishing, 1999

Harmonic Wealth: The Secret of Attracting the Life You Want, by James Arthur Ray, Hyperion Publishing, 2008

Heal Your Body A-Z, by Louise L. Hay, Hay House, 1998

The Law of Attraction: The Basics of the Teachings of Abraham, by Esther and Jerry Hicks (Abraham), Hay House, 2006

Radical Forgiveness, by Colin Tipping, Sounds True, 2009

You Can Heal Your Heart, by Louis L. Hay and David Kessler, Hay House, 2014

ACKNOWLEDGEMENTS

I would like to acknowledge the many people who have helped me and supported me on my own life path to reinventing myself, especially:

Susan Bond, Sharon Burkitt, Julie Curry, Sharon Curtis, Nancy Durand, Tania Griasnow, Rev. Catherine Klein, Rosalyn Pachter, Frances Quintis, the late Judy Sullivan, Susan Walsh, Shirley White, and Robert Wilson, all of whom showed me that I deserve to live my truEST life.

I so appreciate your faith in me.
Trudy

ABOUT THE AUTHOR

Trudy R. Tobias, MSW, LCSW

Having combined counseling, coaching and spiritual practices to reinvent herself, Trudy is on a mission to help other women do the same. She is known for helping women reinvent themselves at any age, guiding and encouraging them to live their truEST* life. Trudy is a life-long learner not only about her profession, but also about herself and her spirituality. From losing an infant at age 38, to becoming a mom through adoption at age 40, to moving to the Southeast from the Midwest at age 57, to changing career directions and leaving a long-term marriage in her 60's, then creating two of her own businesses and becoming an author in her late sixties, Trudy knows personally that it is not only possible to Reinvent Yourself at any age, but also how to grow and thrive in the process! She truly "gets" the struggles and the joys of this process!

In 1971 Trudy earned a Bachelor of Science degree in Education and Sociology from Washington University of St. Louis, Missouri, back in the days before there were bachelor degree programs for therapists. She received her Master in Social Work from Loyola University in Chicago, Illinois, in 1974, and has trouble believing she earned those degrees so long ago! Trudy has worked as a mental health clinician in a variety of settings including family services, middle and secondary level schools, adoption agencies, family and life education agencies, and employee assistance programs, before going into private practice.

As someone who has experienced a lot of changes and transitions in her life and has learned how to thrive, Trudy realized that she wanted to reach out to more women than those in her immediate geographical area to help them do the same. She consequently founded her Transitions Life Coaching business, TruEST* Life Coaching, designed to help women discover their own ability and power to change themselves and their lives for the better. Trudy has been trained in several coaching practices, including Dream Building® and Life Mastery® by Mary Morrissey, Radical Forgiveness® by Colin Tipping, Success Coaching Academy® by Christian Mickelson, and Virtual Coach® by Eben Pagan, in order to coach women anywhere in the world on how to reinvent themselves and lead their truEST life. She also incorporates developing one's spirituality through intuition and mindfulness into her work with clients, and has written this Instructional (Wo)manual, Reinventing Yourself at Any Age to reach even more women.

Trudy grew up and spent most of her adult life in the northern suburbs of Chicago. She listened to her soul and moved to Greensboro, NC, in 2006, at the age of 57, where she lives with her Labrador/Border Collie mix, Odin, and her character of a cat, Binx, in a house full of bright colors that everyone who enters says is a "Trudy-house." Trudy is now the proud grandmother of three grandsons, and through her son-in-law, one granddaughter and great granddaughter. Although Trudy believes she is much too young to be so old as to have grandchildren, she now fully under-stands the plaque that used to hang in her mother's den, "If I had known being a grandmother was so much fun, I would have done it first!" She loves to go to California to visit her family there as well as her family in Chicago as much as possible.

*True Essential Self Transformed

This had been a second marriage for both Darryl and Ilene. Ilene had never had children, and when they met, Darryl's 12 year old son was living with his biological mom in her native Canada, so Darryl and Ilene were able to just focus on one another. While originally Darryl was not particularly successful financially, after marrying Ilene he went up the corporate ladder very quickly. Ilene continued to work as a secretary and moved into an office manager position. Although Ilene was friendly with the women with whom she worked, she did not seek out their friendship after working hours. Nonetheless, she enjoyed her work and for the first time in her life, felt fairly competent. However, after fifteen years in a crowded area near Los Angeles, Darryl convinced Ilene to move to a smaller city that was further south and away from all the places and people Ilene knew.

At this time, Darryl retired from his corporate business and started his own business in real estate. Ilene went to work for Darryl, and she helped him run his business out of their home. Besides taking care of Darryl and becoming an immaculate, if not obsessive, housekeeper, Ilene had no outside interests. She didn't play golf, although they lived on a golf course, for Pete's sake! She wasn't a tennis lady either. Ilene and Darryl belonged to The Club only in order to go to its restaurant. Because Ilene wouldn't drive by herself more than thirty minutes just to do errands, and never traveled to visit family or her former friends without Darryl, her friendships from her former life drifted away and she had made no new friends in the area, preferring to just be with Darryl. Ilene's sister lived with a man whom Ilene didn't like, about two hours away and Ilene would have had to transverse the wonderful California freeway (perhaps parking lot is more accurate) between them, so she didn't see her sister unless Darryl drove her.

At times, Ilene would express sadness and discontent to Darryl, crying for no apparent reason. She could not account for her morose, and never fully explored it. She convinced herself that she and Darryl were blissfully happy in the beautiful home that they had created, and with the business and pleasure trips that they took. After living out in the smaller community for about eight years, Darryl began experiencing some health issues. He slowed down a lot and became reluctant to travel far. After feeling particularly tired for some time, Darryl had an ultrasound which revealed 90% heart blockage. Thus he had that operation and experienced that fateful and fatal heart attack.

Naturally, Ilene experienced deep and profound grief about Darryl's death. Ilene did get help with her grief by going to therapy and joining a widow's group, thereby getting some relief for the intense grief she was feeling. But it was not only grief that Ilene was experiencing. Ilene had become so dependent on Darryl that she didn't know how to manage by herself. She hated staying at home, but also had no one with whom to go out. Ilene felt distraught not only because of missing her husband, but also because she felt her life had no meaning or purpose. She was also filled with anxiety about what the future held even though Darryl had left her well off financially. She truly felt that she had no life now that her husband was gone.

Four months after Darryl's death, and Ilene was still waking up at 2 in the morning, full of anxiety. Her thoughts kept going around in circles: "Something must be wrong with me, I don't know how I can survive without Darryl, I have no life without him, I've never been alone before. I can't sleep, I can't eat, I can't concentrate enough to read anything. I have no hobbies. I've never gone anywhere without him. How will I survive? How am I going to get through this night? Tomorrow will be just as horrible. How will I get through the day? I